Money Rules

Dilemmas in American Politics

Series Editor: **L. Sandy Maisel**, *Colby College*

Dilemmas in American Politics offers teachers and students a series of quality books on timely and key institutions in American government. Each text will examine a "real world" dilemma and will be structured to cover the historical, theoretical, policy relevant, and future dimensions of its subject.

EDITORIAL BOARD

BOOKS IN THIS SERIES

Money Rules: Financing Elections in America

Anthony Gierzynski
University of Vermont

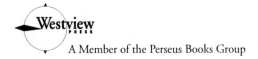
Westview
PRESS
A Member of the Perseus Books Group

Dilemmas in American Politics

Copyright © 2000 by Westview Press, a Member of the Perseus Books Group

Published in 2000 in the United States of America by Westview Press, 5500 Central Avenue, Boulder,
Colorado 80301-2877, and in the United Kingdom by Westview Press, 12 Hid's Copse Road, Cumnor
Hill, Oxford OX2 9JJ

Find us on the World Wide Web at www.westviewpress.com

Library of Congress Cataloging-in-Publication Data

Gierzynski, Anthony, 1961–
    Money rules: financing elections in America / Anthony Gierzynski.
        p.   cm.—(Dilemmas in American politics)
    Includes bibliographical references and index.
    ISBN 0-8133-6860-X (hc)—ISBN 0-8133-6861-8 (pb)
    1. Campaign funds—United States.   2. Campaign funds—United States—History.   3.
Political action committees—United States.   I. Title.
JK1991.G533   1999
324.7'8'0973—dc21   99-049316

The paper used in this publication meets the requirements of the American National Standard for Per-
manence of Paper for Printed Library Materials Z39.48-1984.

PERSEUS
POD
ON DEMAND   10   9   8   7   6   5   4   3   2

For Joseph and Mary Anne Gierzynski

Contents

4 Money in Elections   57

5 Contributors   93

6 Conclusion   115

Illustrations

Tables

Figures

Acknowledgments

This book was built on the work of others and encouraged and supported by others. I'd be remiss if I did not thank them and acknowledge their contributions. First and foremost, I would like to thank the series editor, L. Sandy Maisel, and Westview's acquisitions editor Leo Wiegman for encouraging me to submit a proposal to Westview for this book project. I would not have taken on such a project at this time without their solicitation, and I find myself very thankful that they chose me; I found writing the book for this series very rewarding. I would also like to thank the anonymous reviewers for their helpful suggestions and support of my manuscript.

I would like to thank my frequent coauthor David Breaux and my coinvestigators on the NSF-funded project—Joel Thompson, Gary Moncrief, Keith Hamm, William Cassie, and Malcolm Jewell—and on two Joyce Foundation–funded projects—Paul Kleppner, and Jim Lewis. Without them I would not have had as much experience studying campaign finance, nor would I have had the data for the original research presented in this book. I would also like to thank all of my colleagues who study campaign finance. It is upon their work that this project is built.

For continued support, encouragement, lessons, and insights, I thank my mentors, Malcolm Jewell, Donald Gross, and Robert Albritton.

I would like to thank my students at the University of Vermont as well. Their assistance ranged from discussing campaign-finance issues with me—and in the process helping me to flesh out my ideas—to being a workforce in entering campaign-finance data. Among those students, David Steer, Andrew Pennell, and Andrew Kaplan proved most helpful.

On a more personal level, I would like to thank my daughter, Kelsey, for her patience in sitting in my office while her daddy "did some work on his book," and Lucinda Newman for her personal support and encouragement.

And, finally, I would like to thank the production crew at Westview, including the senior project editor, Kay Mariea, and the copy editor, Bill Kaufman, whose help is just now kicking in, during the last stages of this project.

Anthony Gierzynski

1

....

Introduction

．．

T HE TITLE OF THIS BOOK, *Money Rules,* is a trick, a play on words. So, if you are paging through this book at a bookstore or have just cracked it open after ordering it, now is your chance to reshelve it or return it; for those of you who have been forced to read it for a class, I'm afraid you're out of luck. Like most titles, this one is designed to draw you in, especially those of you who believe simply that "money rules" when it comes to American politics. I know from my experience teaching American politics and reading the newspapers that there are a lot of you out there. In evaluating the American political system it is just so easy to reduce all causes to money, the "root of all evil." If you are one of those people and don't like to be exposed to different perspectives, then you might as well stop reading here and put the book back. If you dare to go further, though, you will see that this book presents a more complicated picture of political reality and the role that money plays in that political reality than is suggested by the cry "money rules."

My goal in the pages of this book is to take the issue of money in politics (or campaign finance) and put it in context: the context of the nature of American democracy and the context of the conflicting political values. By doing so, I believe we can gain greater insight into the issues surrounding campaign finance. In essence, this book is really about money rules (that is, the rules governing campaign finance, not "money rules") and how the behavior that those rules allow affects the health of democracy in the United States.

The 1996 Election: A System in Crisis

From the last week or so of the 1996 election through most of 1997—until the Monica Lewinsky story took over as the press's dominant obsession—the role that money plays in elections became *the* hot topic for the media and those inside the Beltway. The frantic scramble for money and the uses it was put to during the election was revealed in story after story—here are some typical accompanying headlines:

"System Cracks Under Weight of Cash"[1]
"Washington's Priciest B&B: Big Donors Get First-Class Treatment in Clinton White House"[2]

"Oilman Says He Got 'Access' by Giving Democrats Money"[3]
"GOP Hits Gore on Temple Fund Raiser"[4]
"Nuns Tell of Panic About Fund-Raiser"[5]
"Memorandum Suggests that Clinton Made $50,000 Call from the White House"[6]
"An Oval Office Meeting Gets the Asian Money Flowing"[7]
"Chinese Embassy Role in Contributions Probed"[8]
"Democrats Return $1.4 Million in Questionable Donations"[9]

The stories that followed those headlines and others detailed the frantic scramble for campaign money by the Clinton/Gore campaign and the Democratic National Committee in order to fund an extensive air war of "issue ads." (Issue ads are advertisements that ostensibly focus on issues but actually promote or oppose specific candidates.) The Lincoln bedroom was made available to large contributors. Teas were held in the White House to raise money for the issue ads. Buddhist nuns were hit up for contributions during Al Gore's appearance at their temple. The Chinese government allegedly funneled campaign money into the election in order to influence U.S. policy. The secretary of the interior, Bruce Babbit, was accused of reversing a decision on a casino license because of campaign contributions from Native American tribes who opposed the casino. The president and vice president came under fire for fund-raising calls that they made from their offices. Roger Tamraz, a wealthy oilman, testified before the Senate Governmental Affairs Committee that he gave $300,000 to the DNC in order to get access to the White House. He wanted access to the president so he could seek support (unsuccessfully, as it turned out) for an oil pipeline project in Central Asia. Despite failing to get the support he sought, he told the Senate committee that his contribution was worth it and added, "I think next time I'll give $600,000."[10] And Democratic fund-raisers Johnny Chung, John Huang, and Charlie Trie were caught after having raised legally questionable money from various Asian business interests, including the Lippo Group conglomerate owned by the Riady family of Indonesia. The Democrats returned that money and ended up returning $2.8 million overall in questionable contributions from the 1996 campaign.[11]

Some of the fund-raising practices of the Republicans also made the news during that time but were usually lost in the deluge of revelations about the Democrats. The Republican party actually raised more "soft money" than the Democrats and, like the Democratic party, ran "issue ads" to help its nominee, Bob Dole, reach more voters without exceeding the spending limits on presidential candidates. The Republican National Committee (RNC) spent $18 million on "issue ads" that were basically biographical pieces on Bob Dole.[12] Democrats charged the RNC chair, Haley Barbour, with steering $1.6 million from a Hong Kong business to the RNC and state Republican parties through the National Policy Forum. News accounts surfaced of the large sums of tobacco money, both "hard" and "soft," given to the RNC. And the Republican National Committee funneled money to allied interest groups that used the funds to campaign for the Republican cause. For example, the RNC funneled $4.6 million to Grover Norquist's Americans for Tax Reform, which it used to make "4 million phone calls" and mail out "19 million pieces of mail."[13]

After reviewing the campaign practices of the 1996 presidential candidates, Federal Election Commission (FEC) auditors recommended that the Clinton/Gore Campaign repay the government $7 million and that the Dole campaign repay $17.7 million. The auditors "found that the party issue ads" run by the Democratic National Committee in 1995 and the Republican National Committee in 1996 "violated the spending limits of the Federal election laws and should have counted as contributions to the presidential campaigns."[14] A week later these recommendations—which would have represented the largest repayments ever sought from presidential campaigns—were rejected in a unanimous decision by the six members of the Federal Election Commission.[15]

To all appearances it looked as though the system of financing elections—at least at the national level—had gone completely haywire in 1996. The 1996 election seems to have marked the breaking point for a federal campaign-finance system awash in enormous amounts of cash, much of it coming in the form of large and questionable "soft money" contributions. Big contributors were believed to be gaining undue influence over those in power in exchange for their contributions. Candidates, political parties, and interest groups were spending the enormous sums of money on independent expenditures and issue-advocacy advertisements. The leaky dam that had been established to regulate the flow of money had finally collapsed, leaving the regulations that still existed minor obstacles for the cash to flow around.

Meanwhile, the public seemed to not care much about the new revelations regarding the 1996 campaign-finance practices. There seemed to be little outrage or demand for reform.[16] Though no obvious signs of public outrage were evident, polls did show that large majorities of the American public believed that our system of financing campaigns is broken and/or in need of serious repair. In a *New York Times*/CBS News Poll taken in April of 1997, 39 percent of the respondents believed that the system of funding campaigns needs to be completely rebuilt, and another 50 percent of the respondents believed that fundamental changes are needed in the way campaigns are funded.[17] In a survey conducted by Princeton Survey Research for the Center for Responsive Politics (also in April of 1997), 71 percent of respondents thought that "good people being discouraged from running for office by the high cost of campaigns" was a "major problem" for the "federal political system today." Some 66 percent thought that "political contributions having too much influence on elections and government policy" was a major problem. And 61 percent thought that "elected officials spending too much of their time raising money for election campaigns" was a major problem. Even those who contribute to campaigns feel that the system has problems. A survey of contributors to congressional campaigns found that 31 percent of contributors believed that the campaign-finance system is "broken and needs to be replaced," and 45 percent believed that it "has problems and needs to be changed."[18]

Perhaps the public failed to display outrage at the 1996 practices because it was nothing new to them; they had already come to the conclusion that the system wasn't working properly. After all, the issue of campaign finance has long been and will continue to be a prominent story. Journalists have made it a regular habit to do stories connecting PAC contributions to Congressional votes on legislation that concerns the PACs. Every new election seems to bring stories about the "excessive" amounts of money raised and spent in national, state, or local campaigns. In 1998 the "record-setting" spending in the California gubernatorial primaries was the big news (the four serious contenders spent over $72 million).[19] In June 1999 it was the presidential nomination contest. Under a *Washington Post* headline "Bush to Set Record for Campaign Donations," Susan Glasser reported that "Texas Gov. George W. Bush today will shatter the presidential fund-raising record set by the money machine that fueled the 1996 Clinton-Gore reelection, reporting more than $23 million raised in the first half of this year, according to GOP sources, and far outpacing all other White House hopefuls including Vice President Gore."[20] And, long before the emergence of Johnny Chung, White House teas, Buddhist nuns, and so on, other campaign-finance scandals have blared from the front pages. In the 1980s it was the Keating Five, five senators who pressured federal regulators to allow Charles Keating's Lincoln Savings and Loan to remain open, a decision that cost tax payers billions of dollars. Keating had raised large sums of money for each of the five senators through a practice known as bundling. In the early 1990s the questionable practices of GOPAC, the Republican PAC run by Newt Gingrich, were the focus of many news accounts. GOPAC—whose purpose was to assist state legislative candidates—was questioned for its involvement in federal elections without registering with the FEC.

However you look at it—from the perspective of the campaign-finance activities during the 1996 election cycle or from public opinion or from other campaign-finance practices—it is clear something has gone awry in our political system. This is true not just of national elections, but also of state and local contests. But what, exactly, is wrong? What has gone awry? Why do there seem to be so many problems with the financing of elections in the United States? Why do problems seem to keep arising again and again? Why can't something just be done to fix the system?

The purpose of this book is to address these questions in a way that is different from most critiques of campaign finance in the United States. My goal is to create a more sophisticated understanding of the whole issue of campaign finance. I intend to do so by discussing the issue within the context of the U.S. political system and in light of the basic value conflict involved in the issue. Much of the current discourse about campaign finance fails to look at the issue in this way. Instead, the campaign-finance practices are evaluated in isolation from the system in which they take place and without an understanding of the basic conflict inherent in the issue, thus missing what is really critical about the way the role of money in elections affects democracy in the United States.

The problem with campaign finance in the United States is not, as much of the current discourse implies, that money in elections is "bad" per se. Nor is the problem that there is too much money in elections. Nor is it that there are candidates who are willing to shell out enormous amounts of their own money in order to win an election. Nor is it that moneyed interests buy politicians and government policy.

Money Is "Bad," and There Is Too Much of It in Elections

Accounts of the "enormous" amounts of cash in campaigns like the *Washington Post* article quoted above are a regular news item. The subtext of many of these stories is that money is bad, bad, bad, and that more money is "badder." Is money "bad?" Does the absolute dollar value reported in those accounts really mean that there is too much money? To consider these questions carefully, one needs to think of the purpose to which that money is put in elections. If you were to grab a candidate's campaign-finance report and look at what the money is spent on, you might see a list such as that in Table 1.1. Most of what this Democratic candidate for a state senate seat in Vermont spent during the 1996 election cycle was spent on communicating with voters—brochures, advertising in newspapers and on radio, and signs. In general this is the case for most candidates. According to Paul Herrnson, candidates for the U.S. House spent "roughly 76 percent of their campaign funds communicating with voters."[21] A study by Robert Hogan of campaigns for the lower houses of the Texas and Kansas legislatures found that 54 percent of candidate expenditures in the 1998 Texas general election and 81 percent of candidate expenditures in the 1992 Kansas general election were for voter

TABLE 1.1

Itemized expenditures for Ann Cummings, Democratic challenger for Vermont, Washington County State Senate seat, 1996

Date	Paid to	Purpose	Amount
7/19/96	Vermont Federal Bank	checks	$12.00
7/27/96	United States Postal Service	stamps	$39.00
8/27/96	Hull Printing	brochures	$688.00
9/10/96	Hull Printing	ink stamp	$11.00
9/12/96	The Bridge	advertising	$80.00
9/20/96	United States Postal Service	stamps	$13.00
9/24/96	Political Signs Inc.	signs	$202.00
9/30/96	Mail Boxes Etc.	copies	$15.00
9/30/96	Costco	parade	$25.00
10/ 3/96	Valley Reporter	advertising	$94.00
10/ 4/96	The World	advertising	$57.00
10/ 5/96	Aubuchon Hardware	sign posts	$22.00
10/ 6/96	The World	advertising	$115.00
10/10/96	Middlesex Decas	advertising	$48.00
10/20/96	WNES	advertising	$374.00
10/20/96	WDEV	advertising	$416.00
10/20/96	Times Argus	advertising	$115.00
10/20/96	WSKI	advertising	$170.00
10/24/96	WORK	advertising	$414.00
10/25/96	Northfield News	advertising	$37.00
10/26/96	Valley Reporter	advertising	$37.00
10/29/96	Times Argus	advertising	$76.00
10/30/96	WDEV	advertising	$78.00
10/31/96	WSKI	advertising	$91.00
10/31/96	WNCS	advertising	$60.00
10/31/96	United States Postal Service	stamps	$12.00
10/31/96	Times Argus	advertising	$130.00
11/14/96	Mail Boxes Etc.	copies	$6.00
11/14/96	Anne Imbott	advertising	$120.00
11/14/96	The World	advertising	$118.00

Source: Campaign finance report filed with the Vermont Secretary of State.

contact.[22] So the main reason candidates spend money is to communicate their message to voters. Is communicating with voters "bad"? Obviously not (unless, of course, the communications are misleading). Candidates need to buy communications to get their message out and voters need to hear the message in order to make an informed choice at the polls.

So how much should candidates spend trying to get their message to voters? How much is too much? Is the $61.8 million that was allowed the 1996 presidential candidates who accepted public funding enough to reach the almost 200 million eligible voters during that general election? Or even the $140 to $150 million spent to support the Clinton/Gore ticket?[23] That's about seventy-five cents per eligible voter. Compare those numbers to the $100 million the Apple Corporation spent in one week's worth of advertising for its new iMac computer.[24] Should we expect candidates for our most important office to have a smaller budget than that for the iMac? How much should candidates for U.S. Senate races in California spend to reach its 23 million eligible voters?

What is "too much" in these contexts is obviously not all that clear. Yes, some candidates spend what seem like excessive amounts of money. There will always be the Al Checchi types—Checchi spent nearly $40 million of his own money in a losing battle for the Democratic nomination for governor in California in 1998. But aside from such exceptional cases, the average candidate does not spend all that much money, and many candidates, like most candidates who challenge incumbents, spend too little. In the 1998 election the median expenditure for Democratic candidates challenging a House incumbent was $51,760. That means half of Democratic challengers spent less than $51,760. The median for Republican challengers was $71,534.[25] The same is true for most state and local candidates: the big spenders make the news while the typical candidate has to scramble for money. Take California, for example. The average spending by incumbents running for reelection to the state assembly during 1996 was $268,085. The average for challengers? $14,943. That's an eighteen-to-one advantage![26] In Chicago's 1995 election for seats on the city council, eighteen (13 percent) of the aldermanic candidates spent over $100,000, and seventy-two (52 percent) of the candidates spent under $25,000.[27]

Politicians Are Bought, and Corruption Is Rampant

Corruption implies a quid pro quo arrangement; that is, money is given in exchange for political favors. There is no evidence that such arrangements are widespread. There are the occasional cases where an elected official is caught, such as the recent case of Miriam Santos, the Chicago city treasurer, who was convicted for attempting to extort campaign contributions from companies that did business with the treasurer's office.[28] But such events represent a minuscule fraction of all of the campaign contributions. In all the hullabaloo about the 1996 fund-raising practices there has yet to surface any evidence of a quid pro quo arrangement.

The idea that politicians are "bought" is far too simplistic. It is simplistic in its assumptions about why contributors give money, and it is simple in its assumptions about how lawmakers make their decisions. Most contributors desire influence and expect access. But access doesn't always turn into influence—as the case of Roger Tamaraz, a wealthy oilman, demonstrates—and influence can be sought in a number of different ways. Contributors can give to expected winners of elections. They can give to those who exercise a significant amount of power over the policy areas about which they are most concerned. They can give to legislators who have supported them in the past. Or they can give to outsider candidates in hopes of electing a legislator who is predisposed in favor of their cause. And a multitude of factors—including the legislator's own ideology, their perception of their constituents' preferences, their party's position, and the position of the party leadership—affect how lawmakers make their decisions. To boil it down to who gave money to whom is simply a gross oversimplification.

While the simplistic notion of legislators being "bought" is questionable, a more sophisticated understanding of the legislative process suggests that money does come into play in some legislative decisions. While lawmakers are unlikely to vote against their constituents when their constituents care strongly about a piece of legislation, there are many significant pieces of legislation about which the public cares little. And, while some legislation may concern ideological or partisan principles that a lawmaker cares strongly about, there are many that won't. It is in these areas and in the details of the legislative process that those who contribute can have an influence. Methodologically sophisticated studies by political scientists—that is, studies that take into consideration the numerous factors that go into legislators' decision—bear this out. There is little evidence that money influences the votes of lawmakers on key issues on the floor of the U.S. House. But there is evidence that contributions are related to the activity of lawmakers during the legislative process—in committees, where the details of the bills are written—and on issues that do not seem to concern large segments of the population.[29]

Candidates Buy Their Way into Office

This, too, is a gross oversimplification, this time of the electoral process. True, there are the billionaires and millionaires—the Al Checchis, Ross Perots, and Michael Huffingtons—who spend millions of their own money in an attempt to get elected. But, as these cases demonstrate (they all lost), money is not the only factor that determines the outcome of an election. Money *is* important to a campaign's electoral fortunes. In these days of candidate-centered campaigns, most candidates cannot communicate their message to voters without money. Candidates running for presidential nominations need massive amounts of money early in the process to define their candidacy and more in order to stay in the contest.[30] Studies of electoral outcomes in national, state, and local elections have consistently found a positive correlation between money and vote shares.[31] But the nature of the message is also important, as well as the candidate's partisanship and record. You can have all of the money you need to saturate the airways during an election, but if your message does not resonate, or if people are happy with the record of your opponent, or unhappy with your record, you will not likely win. In short, money in most elections is a necessary but not sufficient ingredient for winning. Without it candidates are lost, but with it—even with lots of it—candidates cannot necessarily win unless they are appealing to voters.

Politicians Are Hypocrites

Many critics will accuse politicians of being hypocrites because they argue for reform while continuing to raise money for campaigns. Journalists seem to never fail to point out this "hypocrisy" as illustrated by the following account;

> HOUSTON, Sept. 26—This was the day President Clinton said he has been eagerly awaiting. Finally, after months of foot dragging, the Senate began considering Clinton-backed legislation intended to curb special-interest money in politics. In a speech here this afternoon, Clinton pronounced himself "delighted the debate has begun." And then he headed off to raise another $600,000.[32]

This cynical tone does more harm than good. The fact of the matter is a candidate or party that does not play by the current rules of the game will lose. Unilateral disarmament in campaign finance is electoral suicide. It is pragmatism, not hypocrisy, that leads politicians to play under the current rules while fighting for change. If you don't fight according to the current rules of the game, you *will* lose, and if you lose, you will make no changes.

In sum, many of the problems commonly cited in criticisms of the way the United States funds its elections are neither as bad nor as simple as most people think they are (or as news accounts suggest). It is hard to say whether there is too much money in the system. The claim that politicians are bought is too simplistic: contributions do lead to access and through that access a certain degree of influence, but not in the simple quid pro quo manner that many believe. And, while money does play an important role in determining candidates' electoral support, it is only one of a number of factors that do so; it is a necessary but not sufficient ingredient for electoral success.

The focus on these "problems" diverts attention from the more basic problem created by the current system of campaign finance. And because these problems can be shown to be exaggerated or misleading, the attention paid to them ultimately bolsters the arguments of those who claim that there are no problems with campaign finance and no need for changing the money rules. If, however, we put the way we finance campaigns into its proper context and identify the basic conflict inherent in the issue, the critical nature of the current situation becomes very evident.

The Context

What *is* the proper context of campaign-finance practices? Campaign-finance practices operate under the rules governing them, the money rules. The money rules are part of the overall rules of the game of politics in the United States. And the game is procedural democracy, that is, the democratic procedures followed by the U.S. political system in making law.

How *does* democracy operate in the United States? What democratic procedures does the system follow to give the people a voice in the decisions of their government? Were you to ask some of the people around you, they would probably look at you as though you were stupid and then tell you, condescendingly, that the way democracy works is through elections and majority rule. This view—which is usually tagged as the "majoritarian model" of democracy—is far too simple to capture the nature of the U.S. political system. (In other words, it is they who are the stupid ones.) While the United States does hold elections, U.S. elections operate in a fragmented political system that diminishes their influence. Additionally, elections in the United States do not function very effectively as a means of translating public preferences into government policy. It is rare that elections can bring about wholesale changes in government in the United States because the executive and legislative branches of the national and state governments (both of which hold power in the system) are elected from separate constituencies, at separate times. Additionally, the federal judiciary and some state judiciaries are not elected, nor is the bulk of the bureaucracy at either level. Since 1996, less than half of the eligible voters have actually voted on Election Day. And how that vote is to be interpreted when voters hold many different preferences and political parties are weak is a matter of debate. Parliamentary systems with strong, programmatic political parties are much closer to majoritarian democracies than is the U.S. system.

If not majoritarian, then what? Most political scientists who study American politics believe that the U.S. political system is a pluralistic democracy with a few majoritarian institutions (namely, elections and political parties). A pluralistic democracy is a system in which those with common interests organize into groups in order to influence the course of government. Representation of the public occurs through the competition of these interest groups. Governments in pluralistic democracies are structured so that power is fragmented, which is certainly the case in the U.S. system. A government in which power is fragmented allows interest groups multiple points of access into the policy making process.[33] In the ideal form of this government, interest groups represent all of the concerned interests before government, and the conflict among these groups produces governmental decisions that represent the interests of all concerned. In practice, pluralism in the United States is far from this ideal. Because not all interests are able to organize into groups, and because certain interests have an advantage in political resources (e.g., a large and impassioned membership, skilled leadership, *and* money), the system does not provide for the adequate representation of all segments of society.[34] The two majoritarian institutions in the system—elections and political parties—could make up for this lack of representation, but they do not do a very good job of it, in part because of campaign finance (as I will demonstrate later).

There is a third model of the U.S. political system that many believe describes the system and thus deserves some attention here. It is the "elite model," and it views the U.S. system as an oligarchy, not a democracy. The elite model of our political system suggests that a small political and socioeconomic elite controls our government. This elite exercises its power mainly from behind the scenes. It is a view of our political system that has gained popularity in recent years with shows like *The X Files* and movies like *JFK*. The elite model, however, has some critical flaws, the chief one being that there is no evidence to show that a small socioeconomic elite consistently wins political battles in its favor. Instead, different interests tend to win in different policy arenas.[35] Defenders of the model reply that the lack of such evidence is due to the fact that the elite covers its tracks well—that is, it conceals its influence. But in making such an assertion, their perspective becomes more theological than theoretical. That is, their idea stops being a testable model of a political system and becomes a view that relies on faith, not evidence.

Whichever one of these models you believe best describes the U.S. political system affects your view of the whole issue of the financing of campaigns in the United States. That is because the models set the context for any analysis of campaign financing; they tell us what role political money plays in the system's procedures. A belief that the U.S. political system is a majoritarian democracy leads one to see the private financing of campaigns as corrupting the system because of the large role interest groups play in campaign finance. Any influence interest groups gain via campaign contributions is "bad" in the majoritarian view because interest group influence conflicts with majority rule; minorities (meaning interests that constitute less than a majority of the population) win at the expense of the majority.

A belief that the U.S. system is controlled by a small socioeconomic elite should lead one to conclude that interest-group influence via campaign contributions is only a mirage, because the elite are really running the show from behind the scenes. The fact that most of the money in the political system comes from wealthy interests (which will be demonstrated later) is *not* evidence that supports the elite model. The elite theorists define the elite as a "small" group that operates behind the scenes. While the bulk of contributions come from the wealthy in our society, the notion that those contributors constitute a small group that could work together behind the scenes is absurd.

In a pluralist system, interest group influence via contributions is not necessarily "bad" in its own right. Instead, interest group contributions are part of the natural order of things in a pluralistic democracy, of groups using one of a number of political resources of their members to pressure the government. Influence via contributions *is* a problem when it introduces biases into the system of competition among interest groups. If a resource-based influence consistently tips the balance in favor of certain types of interests in society, then the system becomes biased toward those who have a money advantage.

The most defensible view of the U.S. political system is that it is a pluralist democracy with a couple of institutions (elections and political parties) that could function in majoritarian ways. Given this assessment, my discussion of campaign finance will concentrate on how campaign-finance practices affect the operation of the pluralist system and the operation of the two potentially majoritarian institutions, elections and political parties.

The Basic Conflict

The other key to arriving at a better understanding of campaign finance is identifying the basic conflict that drives the debate over the issue. By identifying that conflict, we can get a sense of how or whether the issue might be resolved. In their American politics textbook, Janda, Berry, and Goldman use the conflict among the values of freedom, order, and equality to explain conflicts over political issues and ideologies in the United States.[36] Criminal policy is understood in terms of the conflict between freedom (civil liberties) and order (absence of crime). Redistributive policies such as welfare are understood in terms of the clash between freedom (from losing income to taxation) and equality (of income or wealth).

The basic or underlying conflict of campaign finance is one that pits two values of great importance to a democracy against each other. Those two values are political freedom and political equality. The conflict between these values originates in the *private* financing of elections, and it plays out in both elections and in the competition between interest groups in the pluralist system. The *freedom* of individuals and groups to spend money on/in political campaigns detracts from equal political representation. It detracts from equal political representation by interfering with the functioning of elections and political parties (key vehicles for equal political representation) and gives financially advantaged interests an upper hand in the interest-group system. Conversely, in order to assure political *equality*, governments need to regulate campaign finance in such a way that restricts the freedom of citizens, individually or as part of groups, to spend their money on political campaigns as they see fit. This conflict between political freedom and political equality is inevitable in a system that relies heavily on private sources of money to finances its elections.

The conflict between political freedom and political equality is rooted in the private financing of elections. Elections present an opportunity for mass participation of a country's citizens in governmental decisions via the selection of representatives or voting on ballot questions. To work effectively, democratic elections require both political freedom and political equality. Candidates and parties must be able to communicate their positions and their record to the voters as freely as possible in order for voters to make an informed and meaningful choice. And, for elections to be democratic, each citizen's vote must be given equal weight (this principle of one-person-one-vote was declared essential to democratic elections by the U.S. Supreme Court in *Baker v. Carr*[37]).

On a small scale the requirements of political freedom and political equality in elections are not so hard to meet. Think, for example, of races in the districts for the four-hundred member New Hampshire House. The single-member districts for this state legislature contain around 2,800 people. On this scale candidates should have no problem reaching most of the voters in the district simply by going from door to door in the district. In this type of campaign, the costs of competing are small. Money is needed to print up literature to leave with the residents, to purchase voter lists from the town clerks, and to cover some of the costs of traveling. The only thing that could keep candidates from competing on an equal footing is their time and ambition. Because campaigning in this type of an election does not require money, the time and ambition of the candidates and the appeal of the candidates and their messages will determine the election, not the amount of money they spend on the election.

The ease of reaching voters via door-to-door campaigning means money is not a prerequisite for communicating with voters. So voters are likely to hear from all serious candidates and thus will be able to make a reasonably informed choice. Furthermore, because candidates don't need to raise money, voters have little reason to suspect that their influence is diminished by the influence of those who give large campaign contributions. For elections with small numbers of voters to reach, then, a high degree of both political freedom and equality can be achieved because in such political races money isn't really necessary.

But contests for the New Hampshire House are not typical of electoral contests in the United States. Most contests for city, state, and national offices involve large constituencies that make door-to-door campaigning impractical and the expenditure of money necessary. State senate districts in California contain about 750,000 people. The median size for state house districts is close to 36,000. Districts for the U.S. House contain about 650,000 people each. Statewide candidates in California have to reach some 20 million eligible voters, in New York close to 14 million. To reach this many voters, candidates need to use forms of mass communication with voters: television, radio, and print advertising; mass mailings; phone banks; and so on. These means of communicating with voters cannot be obtained without spending money, and, in many cases, large sums of money.

When money becomes important to electoral fortunes and when the source of that money is private interests—as is the case for most U.S. elections—political equality and political freedom come into direct conflict with each other. These values conflict because of the unequal distribution of wealth in society and the association between that wealth and certain political interests in the United States. In policy areas such as business regulation, taxation, government spending, and labor policy, those with money often have a common self-interest in the policy— namely, opposition to government regulation and taxation and support for government subsidies for their interests. This means that campaign money will flow mostly to one side in many important policy debates. Government could control the inequalities that result from such a system by limiting the freedom of contributors via regulations on campaign finance. Or the government could provide an alternative source of campaign money, public financing. If government does not restrict the freedom of contributors (or publicly fund elections), the unequal distribution of wealth in society will result in an unequal distribution of money in elections.

An unequal distribution of money in elections leads to unequal political influence by diminishing the role of elections, which in turn makes the interest-group system more important, and, by biasing that interest-group system to favor the financially advantaged interests. In sum, the private financing of elections poses a dilemma for governments: Does the government allow political freedom to spend at the expense of equal political representation? Or does the government limit freedom to protect political equality? In confronting this dilemma, U.S. governments have opted more often than not for the freedom side in this conflict, *and it is this bias that is at the heart of the problems with campaign finance.*

The Problem with the Current System of Campaign Finance

My argument to this point has been that campaign finance operates in a pluralist system with two majoritarian institutions and that it contains a basic conflict between two values critical to a democracy, political freedom and political equality. The problems posed by the campaign-finance systems in the United States are, simply put, the impact of the way the government has resolved the underlying conflict. Specifically, the political system in the United States has tended to favor political freedom to spend at the expense of equal political representation. This choice has negatively affected the operation of elections and consequently has reduced the role that elections and political parties play in the system. The damage done to elections and parties has enhanced the importance of the pluralist mechanism of interest-group competition, whose natural biases are exaggerated by the advantage given to the financially wealthy groups that can funnel significant sums of money into the electoral system.

The wide latitude of freedom to spend allowed in the United States system leads to an unequal distribution of political money in elections. The financial inequalities in elections contribute to the poor functioning of elections and ultimately weaken the role that they play in the democratic system. This occurs because the way that political money is distributed affects the way the vote choice is shaped in an election. Vote choice is affected by the ability of candidates and parties to compete via political communications during elections. The ability to compete and communicate depends upon the amount of money the candidates or parties have, especially in elections with large numbers of voters. If one side lacks money to purchase a sufficient level of communications with the voters, vote choice is diminished because voters do not receive the information required to make an informed choice. In instances where one side cannot even field a candidate because of lack of political resources—and there are many uncontested races in the United States—voters lose their choice entirely. Voter choice is thus shaped in these instances by the decisions of those who contribute to campaigns. This imbalance contributes to the cynicism of the public about elections. So the public stays at home on election day, and the legitimacy of elections as a means of popular sovereignty is called into question.

When those who give out money in elections play a role in shaping the choice in elections, not only do their decisions affect elections but they also become important in the eyes of those who need their money—the candidates and political parties. If contributors are able to use this importance as leverage to influence governmental officials, then they have gained an advantage in the system. They then have more influence than the voters, violating the one-person-one-vote requirement of democratic elections, and they are able to gain an upper hand in the pluralist struggle between interest groups.

The interest-group system in the United States does not do a very good job of providing equal political representation, and the bias toward the freedom to spend in campaign-finance rules makes those biases worse. In 1960, E. E. Schattschneider, in a criticism of pluralism, wrote that "[t]he flaw in the pluralist heaven is that the heavenly chorus sings with a strong upper class accent. . . . The system is skewed, loaded and unbalanced in favor of a fraction of a minority."[38] Schattschneider's critique of pluralism didn't involve campaign finance. He was merely discussing the lack of representation of different interests among organized interest groups at the time. Add the impact of a loosely regulated system of private campaign finance to the system Schattschneider was talking about and you have a system in which it is possible for the wealthy interests to gain an even greater advantage in the political battle. That is the important impact of campaign-finance rules on pluralism. Under the intent of protecting freedom to spend, the United States has created a system of laws that allows an unfettered flow of money from private interests to political campaigns. If the money contributed to campaigns makes the contributors any more influential, then the biases of the system in favor of the most financially advantaged groups grow even worse.

Plan of the Book

The rest of the book will be devoted to supporting the perspective on campaign finance outlined above. In Chapter 2, I will discuss a general model of campaign-finance behavior in order to provide the theory that guides the analysis of campaign-finance practices (the subject of Chapters 4 and 5). In Chapter 3, I will discuss the history of the role of money in elections and the attempts by governments to regulate it. In Chapters 4 and 5, I will use the state of campaign-finance research and data from national, state, and local elections to show empirically the levels of political inequality that exist and to argue why these inequalities matter. The focus of Chapter 4 will be elections. The focus of Chapter 5 will be contributors. In the concluding chapter I will discuss campaign-finance reform in context of the perspective developed here.

Notes

1. Ruth Marcus and Charles Babcock, *The Washington Post*, February 9, 1997, A1.

2. Michael Weisskopf and Charles Babcock, *The Washington Post National Weekly Edition*, January 6, 1997, 6–7.

3. David Rosenbaum, *The New York Times*, September 19, 1997, A1.

4. Ruth Marcus, *The Washington Post*, February 10, 1998, A1.

5. Lena H. Sun and John Mintz, *The Washington Post*, September 5, 1997, A1.

6. Don Van Natta Jr., *The New York Times*, September 23, 1997, A24.

7. Ruth Marcus, *The Washington Post National Weekly Edition,* January 6, 1997, 8.

8. Bob Woodward and Brian Duffy, *The Washington Post*, February 13, 1997, A1.

9. Dan Balz, *The Washington Post*, June 28, 1997, A4.

10. David Rosenbaum, "Oilman Says He Got 'Access' By Giving Democrats Money," *The New York Times*, September 19, 1997, A1.

11. Dan Balz, "Democrats Return $1.4 Million in Questionable Donations," *The Washington Post*, June 28, 1997, A4.

12. Ruth Marcus and Charles R. Babcock, "System Cracks Under Weight of Cash," *The Washington Post*, February 9, 1997, A1.

13. Marcus and Babcock, "System Cracks Under Weight of Cash," A1.

14. Jill Abramson, "Campaign Finance: Audit Faults Clinton and Dole Ads," *The New York Times*, December 2, 1998, A23.

15. Jill Abramson, "Election Panel Refuses to Order Repayments by Clinton and Dole," *The New York Times*, December 11, 1998, A1, A24.

16. R. W. Apple, "Why a Capital Uproar Is a Hinterland Beep," *The New York Times*, March 13, 1997, A25.

17. Frances X. Clines, "Most Doubt a Resolve to Change Campaign Financing, Poll Finds," *The New York Times*, April 8, 1997, A1, A14.

18. John Green, Paul Herrnson, Lynda Powell, and Clyde Wilcox, "Individual Congressional Campaign Contributors: Wealthy, Conservative—and Reform-Minded," working paper.

19. According to the California Secretary of State's Office, candidates for the Democratic nomination—Al Checchi, Jane Harman, and Gray David—spent $38,928,244, $16,380,580, and $8,989,384, respectively. Dan Lungren, the only serious candidate for the Republican nomination, spent $7,701,986. See http://www.ss.ca.gov/prd/finance_98/constitutional_officers.htm.

20. Susan B. Glasser, "Bush to Set Record for Campaign Donations," *The Washington Post*, June 30, 1999, A1.

21. Paul Herrnson, *Congressional Elections: Campaigning at Home and in Washington*, second edition (Congressional Quarterly, 1998), 68.

22. Robert E. Hogan, "Voter Contact Techniques in State Legislative Campaigns: The Prevalence of Mass Media Advertising," *Legislative Studies Quarterly* 22 (1997): 551–571.

23. This figure comes from adding the spending limit in the primary, the public grant of money in the general election, and the money spent by the Democratic parties on issue advertisements and other general campaign support.

24. National Public Radio, *Weekend Edition Saturday,* August 22, 1998.

25. Federal Election Commission, http://www.fec.gov/press/med98.htm.

26. California Secretary of State, http://www.ss.ca.gov/prd/finance96/finance96.htm.

27. Anthony Gierzynski, Paul Kleppner, and James Lewis, *The Price of Democracy: Financing Chicago's 1995 City Elections* (Chicago: Private Money in Local Elections, 1996).

28. Center for Responsive Politics, "Treasurer Convicted of Trying to Extort Campaign Funds," *Capital Eye* 6, no. 3 (May 1999).

29. See, for example, Richard L. Hall and Frank W. Wayman, "Buying Time: Moneyed Interests and the Mobilization Bias in Congressional Elections," *American Political Science Review* 84 (1990): 797–820; John R. Wright, "Contributions, Lobbying, and Committee Voting in the U.S. House of Representatives," *American Political Science Review* 84 (1990): 417–438; Janet M. Grenzke, "PACs and the Congressional Supermarket: the Currency Is Complex," *American Journal of Political Science* 33 (1988): 1–24.

30. Clifford W. Brown Jr., Lynda W. Powell, and Clyde Wilcox, *Serious Money: Fundraising and Contributing in Presidential Nomination Campaigns* (New York: Cambridge University Press, 1995).

31. See, among others, Gary C. Jacobson, *Money in Congressional Elections* (New Haven: Yale University Press, 1980); Alan I. Abromowitz, "Explaining Senate Election Outcomes," *American Political Science Review* 82 (1988): 385–404; Anthony Gierzynski and David Breaux, "Legislative Elections and the Importance of Money," *Legislative Studies Quarterly* 21 (1996): 337–358; Anthony Gierzynski, Paul Kleppner and Jim Lewis, "Money or the Machine: Money and Votes in Chicago Aldermanic Elections," *American Politics Quarterly* 26 (1998): 160–173.

32. Peter Baker, "On Fund-Raising Issue, Clinton Has It Both Ways," *The Washington Post,* September 27, 1997, A4.

33. Robert A. Dahl, *Who Governs?* (New Haven: Yale University Press, 1961); and Dahl, *Democracy and Its Critics* (New Haven: Yale University Press, 1989).

34. See E. E. Schattschneider, *The Semi-Sovereign People: A Realist's View of Democracy in the U.S.* (New York: Holt, Rinehart and Winston, 1960); Mancur Olson, *The Logic of Collective Action: Public Goods and the Theory of Groups* (Cambridge, Mass.: Harvard University Press, 1965).

35. John Heinz, Edward O. Laumann, Robert L. Nelson, and Robert H. Salisbury, *The Hollow Core* (Cambridge, Mass.: Harvard University Press, 1993).

36. Kenneth Janda, Jeffrey M. Berry, and Jerry Goldman, *The Challenge of Democracy* (Boston: Houghton Mifflin Company, 1997).

37. 369 U.S. 186 (1962).

38. Schattschneider.

2

Understanding Campaign-Finance Behavior

I N CHAPTERS 4 AND 5, I will examine the distribution of campaign money in national, state, and local elections and discuss what campaign-finance research tells us about the implications of those distributions for U.S. democracy. The data on the distribution of campaign money, along with the research that has been done to date, are the material that supports my thesis that the problem of campaign finance is the political inequality that stems from the financial inequalities in politics in the United States. Looking at the distribution of money alone, however, does not yield a sufficiently clear understanding of the issue of campaign finance. It is important that we understand the "why" of the distribution of money in campaign-finance systems, the explanation for what we will observe.

The way in which campaign money is distributed in a political system is a result of the interaction between the laws governing campaign finance—which will be discussed in the next chapter—and the nature of campaign-finance behavior—which is the topic of this chapter. Why do people and groups contribute to campaigns? What leads them to give to one campaign over the others? What explains who gets what campaign money and how much they receive? Such questions are questions about the way people and groups act with regard to campaign finance, or campaign-finance behavior. Like most any other behavior, campaign-finance behavior tends to follow certain general principles and is affected by the conditions under which it occurs. It is important to be aware of those general principles and conditions in order to gain a better understanding of how campaign finance works and how money gets distributed in the system.

In this chapter[1] I present a general theory of campaign-finance behavior and focus on what this theory tells us about the distribution of money in campaign-finance systems. I will start off discussing the impact that the setting of the behavior has on the behavior itself. Then I will turn to a discussion of a general principle of campaign-finance behavior that seems to explain a lot of campaign-finance activity, whatever the setting.

The Settings

The general patterns of campaign-finance behavior and the way in which money gets distributed in particular are affected by many aspects of the settings in which they take place. As we will see in the next chapter, the laws regulating campaign-finance behavior vary from federal to state to local elections. These laws affect campaign-finance behavior. There are other characteristics about the settings of these elections that vary, too, and the purpose of this section is to identify them.

In Figure 2.1, I have laid out a model of campaign-finance systems. Campaign-finance systems are, simply, the setting in which campaign-finance behavior takes place. In the United States there are different systems for presidential elections, U.S. Senate and House elections, gubernatorial elections, state legislative elections, and local elections. The model connects characteristics of the setting to campaign-finance behavior—namely, the distribution of campaign money, the levels of spending, the role of money in elections, and the role of money in policy making. In the model I've organized the aspects of the setting that affect campaign-finance behavior into four subsets of characteristics of those systems. The subsets are "election characteristics," "characteristics of the place," "legal characteristics," and "political characteristics."

In the following sections I will discuss how some of the characteristics in each category affect different forms of campaign-finance behavior; I leave it up to the reader to think about some of the relationships that I do not discuss but are suggested by the model. Awareness of how these characteristics affect campaign-finance behavior allows us to understand how that behavior varies from one setting to the next, and such an understanding is necessary given the fact that the United States has many different electoral settings.

Political Characteristics

The political characteristics are the nature of the political environment and political institutions in campaign-finance systems. These political characteristics include the level of party competition, political culture, legislative professionalism, interest-group strength, party-organization strength, the importance of elections, and the degree of decentralization in the policy-making process. Such characteristics affect campaign-finance behavior directly and indirectly.

The level of competition between the two major parties should affect the levels as well as the distribution of campaign funds between the parties. The greater the competition between the political parties, the more active the parties will be in the electoral arena, which, in these days of cash campaigns, means raising more money to support their candidates. If the parties are equally competitive in elections, contributors will likely make contributions to the party with which they agree the most. If one party is dominant, then contributors will give to the members of that dominant party who are most friendly to their interests.

∙∙∙

FIGURE 2.1   Model of campaign finance systems

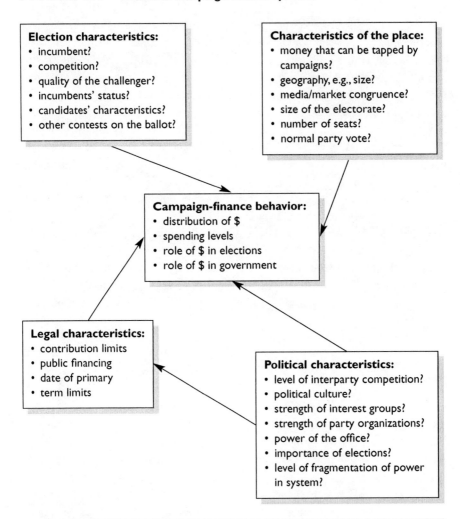

Since interest groups and political parties distribute their campaign resources differently, the relative strength of interest groups and of political party organizations should affect the distribution of campaign money. Because of their interest in access to lawmakers, interest groups tend to contribute most of their money to incumbents. This behavior contrasts with the tendency of the political parties to contribute to candidates in competitive races regardless of incumbency because of their interest in controlling the government. So settings in which interest groups are strong and political-party organizations are weak should have a distribution of money skewed highly in favor of incumbents. In systems in which parties are strong, money should be distributed more broadly among candidates in competitive contests.

Systems with strong political parties may also be settings where candidate spending has less of an impact on elections and on policy making. If party organizations have the wherewithal to provide campaign workers and other campaign resources to candidates (such as phone banks, media consultants, and polling), such resources can increase voter support for the candidate above and beyond the support bought by candidates' spending. In this way party support can make candidates' campaign expenditures less important. Where party organizations can provide such resources, the effect of money from interest groups on policy making will also be diminished. When candidates get a significant amount of help from their political party, they do not need as much interest-group money, and, therefore, the interest groups will have less leverage over individual legislators. Moreover, candidates who get help from the parties can spend less time raising money and thus will have more time to work on legislation.

The power of the office will affect the amount of money raised and the financial advantage of incumbents. One measure of that power in the United States is the professionalism of the office. Professional legislatures, for example, have longer sessions, pay legislators more, and provide research and support staff for legislators. These resources make professional legislators more independent and thus more powerful than their counterparts in less professional (citizen) legislatures. The power and resources make holding a seat in a professional legislature more attractive, so candidates are more willing to pay a higher price for the seat, increasing the cost of elections. The power and resources of a professional legislature also adds to a greater fund-raising advantage for incumbents. Incumbent candidates hold more power in the system because they serve in a more powerful body vis-à-vis other interests and because they themselves are more powerful within that body. So, interests who wish to shape policy will see a greater need to contribute to these types of incumbents.

Political characteristics also influence campaign-finance behavior indirectly by affecting some of the legal characteristics in campaign-finance systems. The political culture of a state, for example, is undoubtedly related to the strictness of campaign-finance regulation in that state. Minnesota, Maine, and Vermont, all with cultural norms that expect clean politics, have adopted tight regulations on campaign-finance practices, including systems for public financing of campaigns.

Illinois, on the other hand, with a culture more tolerant of back-room politics, has practically no limitations on campaign-finance practices, even allowing unlimited corporate contributions. The strength of political parties and interest groups may also shape the "friendliness" of a system's campaign-finance regulations affecting those groups. Where parties are strong, they may create more freedom for their own fund-raising and contributing practices. Where interest groups are strong, they may have more freedom.

Legal Characteristics

Legal characteristics consist of the laws regulating campaign finance—including contribution limits, expenditure limits, public funding, and reporting requirements—and laws setting election practices—including the length of the general election season, term limits, and laws regulating party endorsements.

Campaign-finance systems that do not limit contributions from corporations, political action committees (PACs), labor unions, trade associations, individuals, and political parties may see very different campaign-finance behavior than systems that ban and/or limit certain types of contributions. The absence of limits on contributions will foster higher levels of campaign spending since it is easier to raise campaign funds in larger increments than in smaller increments.

The absence of limits on contributions will also affect the distribution of campaign money. The evidence from research clearly demonstrates incumbents' superiority in raising money from private, nonparty contributors.[2] This superiority comes from the desire of interests to have "access" to lawmakers and from incumbent legislators' aggressive fund-raising.[3] In the absence of limits, private contributors can concentrate even more of their resources on incumbents. Conversely, incumbents in such settings can "hit up" contributors for larger contributions. In such a system, distribution of campaign revenues favors incumbents even more than it would if contributors were legally forced to spread their contributions around.[4]

Large contributions in systems without limits or with relatively high limits also increase the "debt" legislators owe to the interests behind those contributions. Because the larger sums of money give the contributing interest some leverage, such debts have the potential for affecting public policy decisions by legislators. It may even be argued that the maldistribution of campaign funds in systems with no limits may affect public policy indirectly by contributing to low levels of competition in elections, reducing legislative turnover and the responsiveness of representatives to the electorate.

Public funding of elections (that is, providing candidates with government-financed grants) can lead to more equity in the distribution of campaign funds by providing a floor of funding to challengers who traditionally have trouble raising money from private contributors. Public funding reduces candidates' dependence on private money, weakening the possible link between campaign contributions and policy decisions. And public funding can affect the levels of spending in a race if governments use it as an inducement to get candidates to limit their expenditures.

Examples of election laws that have some bearing on campaign-finance behavior include laws specifying the date of the primary (and thus the length of the general-election season), laws allowing for party endorsements, and term limits. The length of the general-election season can affect the importance of money in campaigns. Short election seasons make door-to-door campaigning difficult because there is less time to reach the voters. The need to reach voters quickly increases the value of media campaigns and consequently the costs and importance of money in the election. Laws that allow for party endorsements may affect the distribution of campaign money in primary elections by encouraging contributions to endorsed candidates and discouraging contributions to unendorsed candidates. Term limits may increase the importance of money in elections because of the reduced effect of incumbency: there will be more open-seat contests in which money is more important (see "electoral characteristics") and less accumulation of the personal support that comes with incumbency.

Characteristics of the Place

"Characteristics of the place" are the relatively stable characteristics that set the context of particular races from year to year in a campaign-finance system. Included among these characteristics are the money that can be tapped by campaigns, the geography of the election, congruence between media markets and the geography of the district, the size of the electorate, the number of seats contested, and the normal party vote.

The amount of money that can be tapped by campaigns in a place is determined by the wealth of an area, including the wealth of the citizens and the wealth of interests willing to contribute. These resources of the place affect the amount of money raised and spent in a campaign-finance system. It is unimaginable, for example, that the incredibly high levels of money spent in races for the California Assembly could be raised in a much less wealthy state such as Mississippi. Candidates in poorer areas can raise money outside of their system—and out-of-district fund-raising has become an issue in campaign-finance. Their ability to do so, however, is limited by the interest that contributors have in the candidates' government. If a candidate is running for a state legislative seat in Mississippi and

Mississippi does not make any laws that could concern contributing interests from outside the state, then the candidate will not get contributions from those interests.[5]

The size of the electorate affects the nature of campaigns and thus the importance of money and the cost of elections. Candidates in places with small electorates, such as those that compose the districts for the New Hampshire and Vermont state houses (roughly 2,500 and 3,900 people, respectively) can campaign by going door to door, easily reaching all of the districts' voters while spending little money. Candidates in places with relatively large electorates (such as U.S. Senate and House districts and Florida House districts [with approximately 120,000 constituents]), will find door-to-door campaigning woefully insufficient for reaching all of their districts' voters. Instead they will have to rely more on the mass media, and they will need to skillfully target their campaigns to focus on the voters in the districts that will most likely support them. This type of campaign involves costly purchases for a campaign, including media consultants, air time, computerized data files on the district, and campaign consultants. Not only do such elections cost more, but they are also elections in which money has a greater impact on election outcomes since candidates who have to rely on the other, less costly, means of campaigning will be at an extreme disadvantage.

The geography of an election, meaning the territory covered by the election, can affect the importance of money in elections. Candidates campaigning in districts that cover a large amount of territory will find the costs of reaching voters high because the voters are farther apart. Large districts means more travel time or the use of mass-media campaign techniques, both of which increase costs. The cost of using the mass media will be conditioned by the extent to which mass media reach the voters, a factor that is known as media-market congruence, or the congruence between the media-market areas and the election district. It is very expensive and inefficient for candidates running for office in districts that exist within larger media markets, say a state house district in Atlanta, to purchase mass-media communications. The costs of purchasing advertising time in such markets will be very high, and the candidate will be paying for channels that reach many people outside of his or her district. Candidates running in very large districts will often have to purchase time in several media markets in order to reach voters, thus increasing their costs.

The number of seats in an electoral district is also going to affect the level of spending and the importance of money in elections. While voters in all congressional districts elect only one representative per district, there are a number of states and localities that have districts in which voters elect more than one official.

These multimember districts take on a number of different forms. Some of them are free-for-alls in which all candidates are matched against one another and the top vote getters win the seats. Voters in one state senate district in Vermont (covering most of Chittenden County) cast votes for six candidates from a list of twelve or more candidates. The six candidates with the greatest number of votes win. Some multimember districts have what are known as post positions. Instead of all candidates competing for all seats, candidates face off against one another for one of the seats in the district. Washington State uses such a system for its state house races. In multimember districts candidates will likely be less well known and will be in fiercer competition for voters' attention than candidates in single-member districts. This means they need to spend more money. Candidates in multimember districts will also need to spend more money because multimember districts, by their very nature, would have larger constituencies and thus more voters to reach. These same things that make multimember districts more expensive—candidates being less well known, competition with more candidates with more voters to reach—make multimember districts ones in which campaign spending would be more important for winning.

Finally, the partisan nature of the district—the normal party vote in a district—will affect campaign-finance behavior in a number of ways. Districts where voters are predominantly from one party will not be as competitive from year to year and consequently will be less expensive. Because such seats are safely in the column of one party, they will usually attract little in the way of party or ideological money (key sources of money for challengers). Money is less influential in such lopsided districts since candidates from the minority party will be up against one of the strongest predispositions in voting behavior: voter's political party affiliation.

Electoral Characteristics

Electoral characteristics are the aspects of electoral contests that can vary from one contest to the next within the same campaign-finance system. Since they vary within campaign-finance systems, these are the characteristics that have received the most attention in the extant literature on campaign-finance. Electoral characteristics include the incumbency status of the candidates, the expected competitiveness of the race, the other contests on the ballot, the quality of challengers, the status of incumbents within the legislature, and demographic characteristics of the candidates (such as gender, race and ethnicity).

The presence of an incumbent in a race has an impact on several aspects of campaign-finance behavior. Incumbency affects how much is raised and spent in a particular race. Candidates running against incumbents find it difficult to raise money because, with the close-to-perfect reelection success rates of incumbents, most contributors see challengers' campaigns as lost causes. Incumbents, though they have no trouble raising large sums of money, rarely have to spend it since their competition is often minimal. The rarity of races without incumbents and the greater uncertainty regarding the outcome of such races leads to higher spending levels in these "open-seat" contests. The uncertainty attracts more money from contributors who see a rare chance to use their resources to affect the composition of the government. And, in terms of the candidates, the uncertainty ensures that candidates in these races will spend nearly every dollar that they raise and/or go into debt.

Incumbency also reduces the impact of spending on the vote. Incumbents can use the perquisites of their office—such as consistent media visibility, staff, and free mailing privileges—to build voter support before the election even starts. Challengers, who use campaign money to sway voters to their side, tend to face electorates with favorable predispositions about the incumbent, making it more difficult to win over voters than if voters were unfamiliar with both candidates. As a consequence of these predispositions, spending by challengers has less of an impact on a candidate's vote share than spending by open-seat candidates, and spending by incumbents has the least impact of all.[6]

The expected competitiveness of a race affects spending levels and the distribution of campaign money. Candidate viability is important to fund-raising. Few interests choose to give to candidates who are unlikely to win. In close races both candidates are viable and consequently both will be able to raise relatively large amounts of cash. And, unlike safe incumbents, they will spend almost all of what they raise. Races without incumbents or with strong challengers will be the most competitive and therefore the most expensive.

The expected closeness of the race also affects the distribution of campaign money by affecting the way certain classes of contributors act. Party contributors tend to follow an "electoral strategy." That is, they attempt to effect change through the electoral process by concentrating their resources on close races. By contrast, PACs, individuals, labor unions, interest groups, and corporate contributors tend follow a "legislative strategy." They attempt to influence policy through the legislative process and thus are going to give their money to those candidates who will be in office after the election, that is, the incumbents. So, a greater proportion of money in competitive races will come from the political parties and incumbents in safe races will have more money than they need.

The other contests on the ballot during an election can affect campaign-finance behavior. In election years with big top-of-the-ticket races, such as presidential races or gubernatorial races, much of the money will gravitate toward these contests (if they are competitive), making it more difficult for candidates lower on the ballot to raise funds. Competitive races at the top of the ticket also mean that candidates in other races have to work harder to get voters' attention, thus making spending more important. They may also have to use their funds to fight the coattails of a popular candidate at the top of the ticket.

The amount of power incumbents hold in the system influences the distribution of campaign money. Since money flows to the points of power, officials who hold more important positions—such as legislators who hold leadership or committee positions in their legislature—attract more money because of their influence in the legislative process.[7] The surpluses of campaign funds created by this behavior has, in turn, allowed legislative leaders to create their own campaign committees for assisting legislative candidates and holding on to their leadership positions.[8]

The social and demographic groups candidates belong to affect contribution patterns depending on the resources those groups can mobilize. Women, for example, receive contributions from EMILY's List, the Women's Political Caucus, and, in Minnesota, from the Democratic-Farmer-Labor or Independent-Republican Women's caucuses, as well as from others interested in promoting representation of women in government.[9] The same is undoubtedly true for other demographic groups. It may also be true that certain social and demographic characteristics of candidates depress candidate revenues because of contributor prejudices, though there is little systematic evidence of this.[10]

The context in which campaign-finance activities take place matters. That activity is shaped by the political and legal characteristics of the setting, the place, and the particular election. Awareness of the impact of these characteristics of the setting is crucial to understanding the patterns of campaign-finance behavior. As crucial (or perhaps more crucial) as the impact of the characteristics of the setting on campaign-finance activity is the basic principle that campaign-finance behavior seems to follow: money flows to the points of power.

Money and Power

A key to understanding much about campaign-finance behavior is realizing what purpose money serves in elections. Money in electoral systems is about power—power to influence the course governments will take or, to put it in political-science jargon, power to influence public policy. As a result, money flows to the points of power in the system. This principle is evident when a corporate PAC contributes to incumbent members of committees whose jurisdiction concerns the PAC's parent organization, when corporations and wealthy individuals contribute large sums of money to the political parties' soft money accounts, when an ideological PAC attempts to unseat an incumbent who is "public enemy number one" by running an issue-advocacy campaign, when a political party contributes to challengers or spends on their behalf in order to increase their number of seats in the legislature, when a candidate spends money trying to persuade voters to send him or her to Washington or Columbus, so she can have a role in policy making. The purpose of spending or contributing money is to affect the course of government by creating change among those who hold power in the political system.

Given the principle that money flows to the points of power, identifying the location of power in a political system becomes important in order to follow the money. The location of power in a political system depends in large part on two things: (1) the effectiveness of the elections as mechanisms for policy change and (2) the extent of fragmentation or centralization of power over policy areas. The effectiveness of elections as mechanisms for policy change says a lot about the location of power within a political system. Where elections are an effective means of instituting policy change—that is, where change in control of a public institution is possible and where that change in control means a change in the direction taken by a government—power will reside in elections. Elections that function this way are characteristic of a majoritarian democracy. Consequently, those seeking change will follow an *electoral strategy* by supporting the election of candidates and or parties favorable to the change that they seek. So in this case money will flow to those contestants in elections with whom the contributors agree with the most.

In systems where elections are ineffective mechanisms of change—because public officials are elected from different constituencies at different times and/or because of the difficulty of unseating incumbent office holders—power will reside in the incumbent officials of the regime. In this case public influence on policy must come from lobbying officials of the government—a characteristic of pluralism. Those seeking change in such a system will consequently follow a *legislative strategy*, which seeks to change policy by influencing the decisions of public officials after they have been elected. Under such circumstances, money will flow to incumbent office holders during an election (since they will most likely be the office holders after the election) with less regard for the ideology or specific policy preferences of those office holders than would be the case if elections were more important. The object is to win friends in power and open the way to persuasion after the election is over. This scenario describes the current state of most elections in the United States.

In addition to whether elections effectively lead to change, the relative fragmentation or centralization of power over public policy also helps to shape the flow of political money. In political systems where incumbent officials hold the balance of power and where control over policy areas is fragmented—such as in the U.S. House—money will be directed to the incumbents who have influence over the policy area—committee and subcommittee chairs. In political systems in which elections are most important in determining policy and in which policy control is concentrated—such as in parliamentary systems—money will be directed to the party whose interests are most similar to that of the contributors. In systems where incumbents hold the balance of power and in which power is concentrated—such as state legislatures with strong speakers or strong parties—money will flow to the leader(s) or party holding power. And, finally, in systems where elections are important in determining policy and in which power over policy areas is divided—such as, say, a state agriculture commissioner or state treasurer—money will flow to candidates running for that position who are friendly to the contributors' interests. Figure 2.2 summarizes this reasoning.

So, knowing that money flows to the points of power and knowing where the power resides in a political system, we should be able to predict where campaign money will flow. The U.S. system is one in which elections are not a very effective vehicle for change and one in which power is highly fragmented or decentralized. Consequently, we should expect money to flow mainly to those holding power over the policy area of interest to the contributors, with some consideration for which officials will be the most "friendly" to the interest. This makes the distribution of money in the system different from what it would be if contributors simply followed their ideology or policy preferences. When contributors'

FIGURE 2.2   Power and contributions in political systems

Power Resides in:	Power over Policy Areas	
	Centralized	Fragmented
Elections	contributions to parties based on ideology	contributions to candidates based on stand on policy over which their office would have control
Incumbent officials	contributions to party or leaders in power	contributions to individual incumbents with power over policy realm

ideology and policy preferences coincide with the ideology and policy preferences of those in power, however, the distribution of campaign money should be
the same as when the contributing interests give money based on ideology or
policy preferences. In this situation all money from such contributors will flow
to those holding power over the policy area of concern to the contributors (see
Figure 2.3 for a summary of how money is expected to flow in the U.S. system).
This last scenario is the one that is most dangerous for a political system. If contributors heavily favor one side of a political division and that side is in power, it

. . . .

FIGURE 2.3 **Alternative flows of money when elections are not an**
effective means of bringing about change

A. **Flow of money when contributing interests are aligned with the**
minority party.

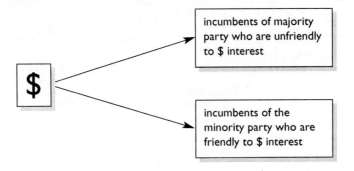

B. **Flow of money when contributing interests are aligned with the**
majority party.

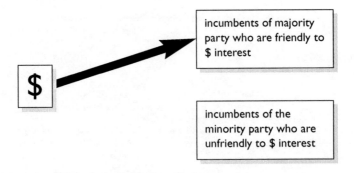

will be difficult for the other side to win power through the electoral process. Such a situation represents the extreme case of how financial inequality can result in political equality.

Conclusion

Money flows to the points of power. Where those points of power are and the role that the money plays is affected by the characteristics of the setting in which the campaign-finance activity takes place. The fact that the legal environments of our campaign-finance systems favors the freedom to spend means that money flows very freely to the points of power within our system, which tend to be incumbent officials and incumbent political parties. This dynamic leads to inequalities among candidates and parties in elections. Whether the resultant inequalities matter depends on how important money is in the elections. The fact that our system allows money to flow freely to the sources of power in our systems also means that those with money have relatively unfettered access to those with power. This creates an inequality of voice that reflects inequalities in the distribution of wealth.

Notes

1. Many of the ideas presented in this chapter have appeared in a previous publication, Anthony Gierzynski, "A Framework for the Study of Campaign Finance," in Joel A. Thompson and Gary F. Moncrief, editors, *Campaign Finance in State Legislative Elections* (Washington, D.C.: Congressional Quarterly Press, 1998).

2. Frank Sorauf, *Inside Campaign Finance: Myths and Realities* (New Haven: Yale University Press, 1992); Anthony Gierzynski and David Breaux, "The Role of Parties in Legislative Campaign Financing," *American Review of Politics* 15 (1994), 171–189; William E. Cassie and Joel A. Thompson, "Pattern of PAC Contributions to State Legislative Candidates," in Thompson and Moncrief, editors, *Campaign Finance in State Legislative Elections*.

3. Sorauf, *Inside Campaign Finance*.

4. Box-Steffensmeier, Janet M., and Jay K. Dow, "Campaign Contributions in an Unregulated Setting."

5. With the growing role of state governments in making policy (a trend that has been in place since the beginning of the devolution period in the 1980s), the actions of state governments *have* been of concern to many out-of-state interests. Consequently, the amounts of campaign money in many states has increased significantly; a likely source of that increase is out-of-state contributors.

6. Anthony Gierzynski and David Breaux, "Legislative Elections and the Importance of Money," *Legislative Studies Quarterly* 21 (1996), 337–358.

7. Box-Steffensmeier and Dow, "Campaign Contributions in an Unregulated Setting"; Kevin B. Grier and Michael C. Munger, "Comparing Interest Group PAC Contributions to House and Senate Incumbents," *Journal of Politics* 55 (1993), 615–643.

8. Ross K. Baker, *The New Fat Cats: Members of Congress as Political Benefactors* (New York: Priority Press Publications, 1989); Anthony Gierzynski, *Legislative Party Campaign Committees in the American States* (Lexington: University Press of Kentucky, 1992).

9. Anthony Gierzynski and Paulette Budreck, "Women Legislative Caucus and Leadership Campaign Committees," *Women & Politics* 15 (1995), 23–36.

10. Barbara C. Burrell, "Women's and Men's Campaigns for the U.S. House of Representatives, 1972–1982," *American Politics Quarterly* 13 (1985), 251–272; Carole Jean Uhlaner and Kay Lehman Shlozman, "Candidate Gender and Congressional Campaign Receipts," *Journal of Politics* 48 (1986), 30–50; Robert E. Hogan and Joel A. Thompson, "Minorities and Campaign Contributions," in Joel A. Thompson and Gary F. Moncrief, editors, *Campaign Finance in State Legislative Elections* (Washington, D.C.: Congressional Quarterly Press, 1998).

3

Elections, Campaign-Finance Law, and Public Opinion

In CHAPTER 1, I argued that the private financing of campaigns creates a dilemma for our political system: should our system promote political equality by restraining spending on political messages, or should we promote political freedom qua spending and ignore the inequalities that result? I have also argued that in resolving this conflict, our political system has opted for campaign-finance systems that are heavily biased in favor of freedom to spend at the expense of political equality. This bias toward freedom to spend is true of campaign-finance laws that regulate federal elections and most of the laws that regulate state and local elections.

How did our campaign-finance systems come to so heavily prefer freedom to political equality? How did this tension between political freedom and political equality become part of our elections in the first place? Has it always been this way? The purpose of this chapter is to answer these questions by delving into the history of elections and campaign-finance law, and by looking at the status of public opinion on campaign finance. Since the role of money in elections is the source of the tension between political freedom and political equality, I will examine the history of elections to trace how money came to play its important role.

Money in Elections

Before sound bites, negative ads, spin control, issue ads, media consultants, campaign consultants, and so on—that is to say, before the modern age of electoral politics—campaigns were, to state the obvious, very different. From the nineteenth to the midtwentieth century, elections were party-centered, meaning that electoral campaigns were run by the party and for the party. The political parties controlled who would run for office. They amassed the volunteers. They campaigned for their candidates. And they mobilized the voters. The point of it all was for the party to gain or maintain control of the government. Candidates in party-centered elections depended mainly upon the strength of their party to get votes on election day. Voters loyally supported the political parties, tending to cast votes for the same party each election.

Victory on election day depended upon mobilizing an army of party workers at the grassroots level in order to turn out the loyal party voters. The political parties used money to cover various expenses associated with grassroots campaigns—e.g., paying party workers, printing campaign material, and sometimes even buying votes. Elections, however, were won through the work of the party organization, not by the expenditure of money on expensive campaign ads, hired campaign consultants, or pollsters.[1] The party officials determined the strategy, and the precinct captains kept them abreast of "public opinion" and spread the party message.[2]

The conflict between freedom to spend and political equality in the private financing of campaigns began to surface near the end of the age of party-centered campaigns.[3] With the demise of parties' central role in elections, the advent of the electronic media, and the development of modern campaign tools, campaign money increased in importance. As money became more important to the success of electoral campaigns, the conflict between political equality and the freedom to spend intensified.

Around the turn of the century—partly in response to the effectiveness of urban Democratic machines in empowering city populations of recent immigrants and partly in response to the widespread corruption in those machines—political parties became the targets of Progressive reforms that severely reduced the parties' role in elections. Perhaps the most devastating reform—adopted widely and quickly in the early 1900s—was the direct primary. Under the direct primary system, instead of the parties selecting who would run under their labels, voters chose the parties' nominees in primary elections. The loss of control over those who would carry the party's banner into the election meant a loss of control over the party's message.

Additionally, the advent of the direct primaries made the political parties less important as electoral machines. Primaries made it necessary for aspiring candidates to build their own campaign organization and raise money themselves. Parties could not, from a practical or legal standpoint, provide organizational or financial help for candidates.[4] Once candidates built their own organizations, there was little incentive to dissolve those organizations and allow the party organization to take over for the general election. After all, the candidates exercised complete control over their own organizations; they did not control the party organization. Consequently, party organizations qua campaign organizations were shoved toward the sidelines of election contests, and election campaigns eventually became campaigns run by the candidate, financed by funds raised by the candidate, and operated for the purpose of electing the candidate.

Other changes in our political system weakened the political parties by weakening the attachment voters felt toward the parties. The rise of the welfare state during the New Deal and civil service reform reduced the ability of the political parties to offer something tangible to voters for their loyalty. In urban areas the political parties often provided many of the services that government agencies now provide. New immigrants to the cities were greeted by the party's precinct or block captains, who provided services that helped the immigrants get on their feet—food, shelter, and, ultimately, jobs with the city or county government. Many immigrants were assimilated into our democratic system and empowered politically in this manner. As you might expect, this assistance engendered a great deal of loyalty to the party that registered in election results. The expansion of the federal welfare state that began under the New Deal, however, meant that government displaced the political parties as welfare providers, thus depriving parties of this means of generating loyalty. And the development of civil-service laws further eroded the political parties' ability to reward loyalty by taking away patronage jobs. Patronage jobs were government jobs awarded by victorious parties to party supporters. Civil-service reforms ended most patronage by insulating government workers from political pressure, making government employment more a function of merit.

But partisan loyalty wasn't all based upon tangible, material benefits provided directly to prospective voters. Loyalty was also based on a history of party performance and party platforms, and it was the rise of television as a medium of communication that eroded this basis of party loyalty. Television allowed candidates—for a price—to reach the voters directly, bypassing the party organizations. Candidates could (and did) make their appeals directly to voters, often without any mention of the party. (Next election time check candidate advertisement for references to the candidates' political party within the ad—you will find them to be quite scarce.) Additionally, television is a medium of images. It is best at conveying images of persons; it cannot effectively convey images of a party's performance or platform. So the focus of politics in the age of television becomes the person, not the party; that is, the character and the personality of the candidates as gleaned from television appearances as opposed to issues that divided the political parties. Party performance and platforms become less relevant, weakening voters' attachment to the political parties. With weakened partisan attachments, voters become more susceptible to the attempts at persuasion transmitted by the candidates or other groups via potentially expensive mass-media campaigns.

The direct primary, the rise of the federal welfare state, civil service reforms, and the development of television have all worked together to weaken U.S. political parties and transform our elections into candidate-centered campaigns that require much more money than the party-centered campaigns of the past. Money

POLITICAL PARTIES TODAY

Political parties are not out of the picture in U.S. elections today. Parties no longer slate the candidates or run the campaign machinery, but they do provide some electoral services to candidates, and they do raise money and help candidates raise money.[5] By all indications from the 1996 election, they can raise lots of money (see Chapter 4). When they do so, however, it is for the purpose of furthering its candidate's fortunes, not some general party platform. A recent court ruling that allows parties to make independent expenditures for or against candidates, however, may reintroduce general party campaigning.

It is also important to comment on the uniqueness of the U.S. electoral system when compared to other democracies, which have maintained more party-centered elections even in this modern age of electronic communication. Parties in other countries still pick their own nominees. In fact, the United States is the only democracy that uses primary elections. The effects of television are limited because most other democracies have laws that ban candidates from running television advertisements. In Britain, for example, the party is given free air time, and candidate ads are prohibited. As a result, money plays less of a role in these more party-centered systems.

is needed to build and maintain a campaign organization; to hire and pay campaign experts—pollsters, campaign consultants, media consultants, and fund raisers to raise more money; and to purchase communication with voters.

As I argued in Chapter 1, fulfilling this need for money in modern campaigns creates a dilemma for our political system. When candidates turn to the private sector to raise this money, the unequal distribution of economic resources in the private sector gets translated into an unequal distribution of political resources in the electoral arena. Recognizing this problem, Congress, state legislatures, and city councils have over the years tried to regulate campaign finance.

A Brief History of Campaign-Finance Regulation

As early as 1904—when elections were still party-centered—concern was raised about influence bought by large contributions to the political parties. This concern led to a ban on direct corporate political contributions for federal office under the Tillman Act of 1907. In 1943 the same concern led to a ban on contributions from the treasuries of labor unions under the Smith-Connally Act. During this period Congress also enacted other laws—in amendments to the Tillman act, the Corrupt Practices Act of 1925, and the follow up to the Hatch Act of 1939—that required disclosure of the finances of federal candidate and party committees and even put limits on what campaign committees could spend. The disclosure requirements and the limits were ineffective at best; there was no enforcement, and skirting the limits took little imagination. Whether the regulations were effective or not, the intent of all of these early attempts at regulating campaign finance was to address the corrupting influence that money can have on elections. Large political campaign contributions were believed to be corrupting the system by giving those who contributed undue influence over government policy.

But it wasn't until our elections had evolved more fully into candidate-centered contests that a comprehensive and concerted attempt to regulate campaign finance was put into place. By the 1960s the amount of money spent in federal elections was rising dramatically and, along with it, concern about the impact of that money on the political system. The concern led to the passage of Federal Election Campaign Act (FECA) in 1971. The act placed limits on the amount candidates could contribute to their own campaigns and limited media expenditures. The act also required strict disclosure of the campaign-finance activities of candidates and political committees.[6]

The FECA of 1971 operated for one election before Watergate generated additional concerns about campaign finance that led to more comprehensive reform. The investigation into Watergate revealed major campaign-finance abuses by Nixon's Committee to Re-elect the President (CREEP) during the 1972 election. CREEP was found to have accepted excessively large contributions, to have laundered campaign money, and to have accepted illegal contributions from corporations. It was alleged that those who made these large contributors received or were offered ambassadorships and/or legislative favors.[7] Additionally, Nixon's campaign organization was found to have maintained undisclosed slush funds, secret safesful of cash to pay for certain beneath-the-board campaign expenses. (The burglars that broke into the headquarters of the Democratic National Committee in the Watergate office building were paid out of such a slush fund.)[8] The disclosure of these activities naturally led to heightened concern about campaign finance. Those concerns led Congress to pass the 1974 amendments to the FECA.

The 1974 amendments represented a much more comprehensive attempt at controlling the influence of money in elections than the 1971 Act. Limits were placed on the size of contributions, the amount candidates could contribute to their own campaigns, and the level of campaign expenditures by candidates and other groups. A system of public funding was created for presidential contests. During the presidential nomination campaign candidates would be given matching funds for small contributions if they adhered to state-by-state and overall expenditure limits. The candidates who won their party's nomination for president and accepted the public funds (amounting to $61 million in 1996) had to limit their campaign spending to those funds during the general election. The 1974 amendments to the FECA were an aggressive attempt at restoring some accountability and equality in our elections and they did so at the expense of those who wished to spend their money freely in elections. The U.S. Supreme Court, however, did not allow this situation to stand for long.

In 1976, before the 1974 amendments could take effect, the Supreme Court in the case *Buckley v. Valeo*[9] invalidated much of the new campaign-finance law. The Court struck down the FECA expenditure limits because a majority of the justices found that the spending limits violated the First Amendment's freedom of speech clause. In the words of the court,

> A restriction on the amount of money a person or group can spend on political communication during a campaign necessarily reduces the quantity of expression by restricting the number of issues discussed, the depth of their exploration, and the size of the audience reached. This is because virtually every means of communicating ideas in today's mass society requires the expenditure of money. . . .
>
> The expenditure limitations contained in the Act represent substantial, rather than merely theoretical, restraints on the quantity and diversity of political speech.

In essence, the Court, recognizing the importance of money in today's elections, equated the expenditure of political money with speech and thus put it under the protection of the First Amendment's freedom-of-speech clause. Consequently, expenditure limits were ruled unconstitutional, and so were any limits placed on candidates' contributions to their own campaigns. (See Figure 3.1 for a summary of the law before and after the Court's ruling.) Just as important, the court, in its discussion of the issue, explicitly rejected political equality in elections as a legitimate reason for government to interfere with this protected freedom to spend.

In subsequent cases the judiciary struck down other laws that interfered with political spending, including many provisions of state campaign-finance laws that were enacted in the wake of Watergate and the FECA. From the *Buckley* case on, the court's position that political spending equals speech has been their guiding principle in campaign-finance cases, leading them to invalidate many other campaign-finance regulations. In *First National Bank of Boston v. Bellotti*[10] (1978), for example, the court ruled that states could not regulate spending for or against voter referenda. So corporations (as in this case) or other interests are free to spend as much as they wished to support or oppose ballot measures. More recently, in 1996, the court ruled in *Colorado Republican Federal Campaign Committee v.*

• •

FIGURE 3.1   Campaign-finance law before and after *Buckley*

Federal Election Law with 1974 Amendments to the FECA

• Limits on expenditures by
  • candidates
  • groups operating independent of candidates
• Limits on contributions
  • by PACs, individuals, and political parties
  • from candidates to their own campaigns
• Public funding for presidential candidates during the primary and general elections
• Established the Federal Election Commission (an independent agency)

Federal Election Law after Buckley *Ruling:*

• ~~Limits on expenditures by~~
  • ~~candidates~~
  • ~~groups operating independent of candidates~~
• Limits on contributions
  • by PACs, individuals, and political parties
  • ~~from candidates to their own campaigns~~
• Public funding for presidential candidates during the primary and general elections
• Established the Federal Election Commission (an independent agency) FEC reconfigured by 1996 Amendments

---

Federal Election Commission[11] that Congress could not regulate independent expenditures made by the political parties for or against candidates. And in 1998 the Supreme Court let stand two more rulings by lower courts that overturned spending limits for Cincinnati City Council elections and *contribution* limits in Arkansas.[12] In the Arkansas case the U.S. Court of Appeals for the Eighth Circuit ruled that the state's three-hundred-dollar limit on contributions to candidates for statewide offices and the hundred-dollar limit on contributions to legislative candidates were too low.[13]

It is difficult to overstate the impact of the court's decision in *Buckley*. Its zealous protection of the freedom to spend has made it nearly impossible to regulate campaign finance for the purpose of promoting political equality in elections. It, more than anything else, is the reason our system so heavily favors freedom to spend in our private system of financing elections. Under its watchful eye, regulation of campaign contributions is permissible. Those limits, however, cannot be too low, as Missouri, Oregon and Minnesota found. The courts struck down the hundred-dollar contribution limits they had enacted in the 1990s.[14] Limits on expenditures are out of the question unless they are voluntary. The only way governments have been able to coax candidates into following voluntary spending limits is by introducing public money in elections: governments can offer public funds for election expenses in exchange for an agreement by the candidates to follow the limits. Serious public funding programs with spending limits are, however, very difficult to enact and effectively maintain. They fall easy prey to opponents who label it "welfare for politicians." Without a public-funding mechanism, limits on how much money candidates can contribute to their own campaigns are out of the question, too. And even with public funding, limits on independent expenditures and on spending on issue campaigns are out of the question.

Since the *Buckley* case, Congress has revisited the issue of campaign finance many times, but only once did it actual make any change in the law. In 1979 it amended the FECA to allow state and local parties to carry out grassroots activities—such as registration and get-out-the-vote drives—that benefited federal candidates indirectly without those activities counting as contributions to the candidates under the FECA.

While the federal law stood still, more court rulings, advisory opinions by the Federal Election Commission (FEC), and the development of creative fundraising practices have eroded the effect of the FECA even further. The combination of the 1979 amendment to the FECA and an FEC advisory opinion opened the door to "soft money." Essentially, soft money is unregulated money raised and spent by the political parties. As stated above, the 1979 amendment to the FEC excluded the costs of carrying out general campaign activities from the limits on party contributions to candidates. An advisory opinion by the FEC allowed money raised above and beyond the limits of the federal law to be used to cover the nonfederal portion of the general campaign activities of the national parties.[15] This ruling meant that the national parties could raise unlimited amounts of money—including from corporations and labor unions—and use that money to defray their administrative costs and transfer it to the states, where it would be used for general campaign purposes (as long as the contributions were legal under state law). The soft-money option for the parties in effect allowed unregulated money to flow back into federal elections. The national party committees jumped on this opportunity, raising large sums of soft money. In 1996 the Republican's national committees raised $141.2 million. The national Democratic committees raised $122 million.[16] They used the money to run "issue ads" that benefited their presidential nominees; they distributed the rest to state party organizations that registered voters, campaigned on behalf of the parties' candidates (both state and federal), and got voters to the polls on election day. In the 1998 midterm election, the party committees of the Democrats raised $89 million in soft money, the Republican committees $111.3 million.[17]

The court's protection of political spending under the First Amendment has also opened the door to "issue advocacy." Money spent advocating an issue position is, according to the judiciary, beyond the reach of federal regulations as long as the issue advertisement does not directly and explicitly advocate the election or defeat of a candidate.[18] Issue advocacy, like soft money, has opened the door to massive amounts of money unregulated by federal election law (and unreported as well). It has been estimated that approximately $135 to $150 was spent on issue advocacy during the 1995–1996 election cycle.[19] The 1997–1998 election cycle saw approximately $275 to $349 million in issue-advertising spending.[20]

In addition to soft money and issue advocacy, candidates and fund-raisers have used a variety of techniques to get around the federal law. Individuals or groups that wish to avoid limits on what they can contribute to candidates have followed the practice of "bundling," a technique by which one person or group gets others to write checks to a candidate. The checks are bundled, and the fund-raiser presents them to the grateful candidate. EMILY's List is an organization that bundles money for female candidates.[21] Another example of how candidates have developed ways to skirt the limits of federal law is detailed in Anthony Corrado's book *Creative Campaigning*.[22] In it he describes how presidential candidates avoid spending and contribution limits of the public-funding system for the primaries and caucuses by setting up preelection committees.

In sum, federal law, as I suggested in Chapter 1, has essentially been reduced to rubble, rubble that is ineffective at stemming the flow of money into federal elections. Figure 3.2 depicts the options open to money flowing into the system.

While the federal government has stood still, state and local governments, motivated by public concerns over the growing importance and influence of money in *their* elections, have been much more active. Michael Malbin and Thomas Gais report that "[a]bout two-thirds of the fifty states have enacted major new campaign finance laws since . . . 1979."[23] Those reforms have ranged from increasing disclosure requirements to establishing total public-funding systems and have included some new ideas as well as the standard limits on contributions from individuals, parties, and other political organizations. Oregon, for example, restricted the percentage of money candidates could raise outside of their district. Minnesota attempted to control the impact of independent expenditures by adjusting the public funds and spending limits for candidates in reaction to independent expenditures made on behalf or against a candidate. Missouri prohibited incumbents from carrying over excess campaign funds from the previous election. And Maine and Vermont enacted public-funding systems that attempt to eliminate private money from elections.[24]

FIGURE 3.2   How big $ finds its way into federal elections

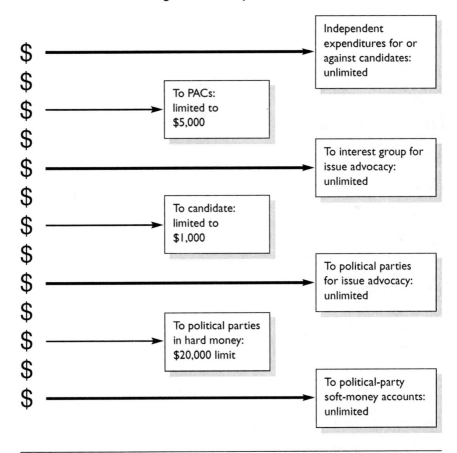

(Explanation: Arrows represent options for individuals who wish to use their money to influence the process. Wider arrows indicate that more money can flow through that route.)

The two largest cities in the United States have enacted reforms as well. New York City (in 1988) and Los Angeles (in 1990) adopted systems of public funding for city candidates with corresponding spending limits. Qualified city-council candidates in both cities receive public funds to match contributions of a certain size, and in exchange the candidates must abide by spending limits.[25]

Many of these new ideas, however, are either being challenged or have been invalidated by the courts because they infringe upon the freedom to spend that the courts say is protected under the First Amendment. The courts have struck down Oregon's limit on out-of-district (or state) contributions and Minnesota's attempt to control independent expenditures. The courts also struck down Missouri's attempt to limit incumbent advantage by preventing the carryover of funds from the previous election.[26] And the Maine and Vermont laws are currently being challenged in the courts.

The Status of Campaign-Finance Laws Today

So where does all of this leave us? It leaves us with elections in which the freedom to spend is well protected while governments are hamstrung in their attempts to ameliorate the inequalities created by the system of privately financed elections. The U.S. Supreme Court has set the framework within which any attempt to regulate campaign finance must operate. Because campaign spending, in the eyes of the court, is equivalent to speech, campaign-finance regulations must pass a very strict standard before they are allowed to impinge upon the freedom to spend. Promoting political equality is not, according to the courts, a valid reason to interfere with the freedom to spend. Governments are thus hampered in their attempts to assure equal political representation. The only effective tool that the courts have allowed to stand is public funding of campaigns.

Because the national government, state governments, and some local governments have tried different approaches to regulating campaign finance, we do have some variety in campaign-finance laws in the United States. The campaign-finance systems created by these laws are all constrained by the spending-equals-speech principle of the *Buckley* ruling, but it is still worthwhile to note that there are differences; some systems do place some restrictions on freedom in an attempt to maintain a certain level of political equality. To illustrate this, I present a map of the campaign-finance laws in the fifty states in Figure 3.3. The states are shaded according to how their laws make the tradeoff between freedom to spend and political equality.[27] States with no shading have opted for complete freedom to spend, placing few restrictions on campaign finance behavior—usually just reporting requirements. The states shaded with black are the states with the strictest campaign finance laws, involving public-funding systems with corresponding restrictions on campaign expenditures. The law for federal elections would, according to my scoring, gets a "2."[28]

One can see from the map that most of the states favor freedom to spend when it comes to campaign finance. Twenty-six of the states were rated either a "1" or a "2." Of those, eleven states, including some of the most populous states—California, Texas, and Illinois—allow for almost unlimited freedom in campaign-finance

••

FIGURE 3.3   **Freedom versus equality in state campaign-finance laws**

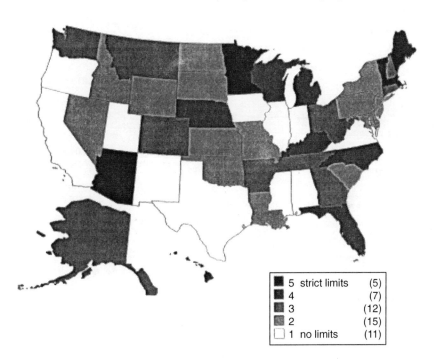

■	5 strict limits	(5)
■	4	(7)
■	3	(12)
▨	2	(15)
☐	1 no limits	(11)

Source: Edward D. Feigenbaum and James A. Palmer, *Campaign Finance Law 98* (Washington D.C.: Federal Election Commission, 1998); updated by news accounts of recent changes in the law.

activity. Only five states—four of which are northern, politically liberal states— had laws that strongly promoted political equality. With the exception of Minnesota, each of these states has only recently adopted these laws, so they have yet to be tested in the courts; and, given the courts' history, it is highly likely that it will strike them down. The rest of the states mix and match limits and prohibitions on contributions, none of which, according to the study by Malbin and Gais, are very effective at promoting equality in elections.[29]

Public Opinion on Campaign Finance

Where does the public stand on campaign finance? Though the key decision on campaign finance has come from the U.S. Supreme Court—the branch of government that is most insulated from public pressure—public opinion is still important on this issue. It is important in the sense that public opinion can at least be said to set the general boundaries for what is acceptable in election financing or governmental regulation of campaign financing. Additionally, the absence of strong and united public opinion can be significant, too, since sustained solid public support for reform would probably put enough pressure on governments to change the current way elections are financed through options still allowed under *Buckley*.

Before getting to specific opinions about campaign finance, some comments about the general political culture are useful in understanding public opinion on this issue. The conflict between political equality and political freedom at the core of campaign finance echoes the tension between these two values, which others have identified as an integral part of our political culture.[30] This tension is manifested in public opinion on economic and social policy and is sometimes resolved by defining equality as equality of opportunity, not equality of result. This resolution doesn't work when it comes to political equality, however, because *elections require equality of result*. For elections to be democratic—that is, to be an institution that ties majority public sentiment to governance—political equality of result is necessary; each person's vote must count equally. This notion of equality of voice is what the public wants as well.[31] So we should expect to see the unresolved tension between demands for equality and freedom in elections manifested in some ambivalence with regard to opinion on campaign finance.

In Chapter 1, I presented poll numbers that show that in 1997 there was public consensus that something is wrong with how elections are financed in the United States. What the public thinks should be done about it, however, is not so clear. A survey taken in April 1997 found that 57 percent of respondents favored banning all private contributions and using government funds to pay for campaigns.[32] That is, a majority favors ending the system of private financing and establishing a system of public financing of campaigns! But 47 percent of the respondents in the same survey favored "removing all limits on campaign contributions, provided that campaigns make known who donated the money and how much they donated." That is, close to a majority favors a completely free and unfettered privately financed system.[33] Clearly some respondents are opting for both the equality and the freedom sides of the issue of campaign finance. For the opinion on some other reforms, see Figure 3.4.

These contradictions demonstrate an ambivalence on the part of the public with regard to how they view the financing of campaigns. It is an ambivalence that is most likely a reflection of the underlying tension between political equality and freedom in our culture. In essence, the public wants both. This ambivalence

FIGURE 3.4   Public opinion on campaign-finance reform proposals

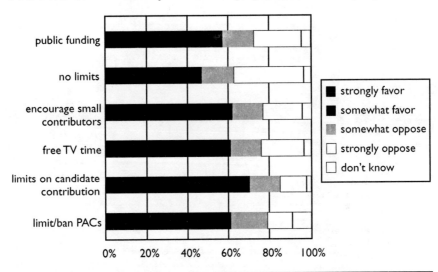

I'm going to read you some different proposals to change the way federal election campaigns are run. As I read each proposal, tell me if you would strongly favor it, somewhat favor it, somewhat oppose it, or strongly oppose it. How about this proposal?

Source: Created by author from the results of the *Money and Politics Survey,* Princeton Survey Research Associates.

also sends mixed signals to lawmakers about campaign-finance reform and perhaps accounts for the failure of lawmakers at the national level to change the system in recent years. I suspect that the states that have been active have been so because the views of the state public are more clear-cut. Some state cultures are much more supportive of the use of government to promote equality in participation than others. Indeed, the states that have been the most successful in attempting to address the inequalities in the system are states with such relatively liberal cultures—Maine, Vermont, Massachusetts, and Minnesota.

In addition to ambivalence about solutions, the public doesn't give the issue of campaign finance much priority. When asked "how much of a priority would you like to see the president and Congress give to reforming the campaign finance system," 15 percent answered "top priority," 45 percent "high priority."[34] Those results seem high, but campaign-finance reform's priority relative to other issues is rather low. Only 18 percent gave it priority over balancing the federal budget;[35] 12

FIGURE 3.5   **Public opinion on priority of campaign-finance reform**

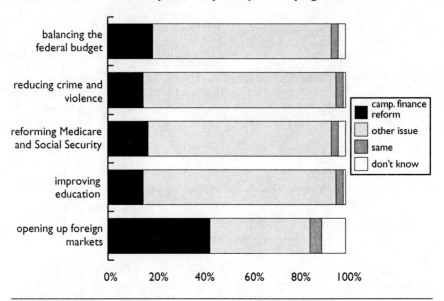

We'd like you to rate campaign finance reform as a priority for the president and Congress compared with some other issues. Which should have a higher priority this year—campaign finance reform or . . .

Source: Created by author from the results of the *Money and Politics Survey,* Princeton Survey Research Associates.

percent gave it priority over "improving education." And these results are from a survey taken during the height of revelations about the questionable campaign-finance practices of the 1996 election! Clearly, the fact that the public doesn't give the issue of campaign finance a high priority, along with the ambivalence with regard to what should be done, helps to maintain the status quo, which favors the freedom to spend.

Summary

U.S. elections have evolved in such a way as to make money an important part of campaigns. The decline of the political parties, the rise of candidate-centered campaigns, and the subsequent need to use the mass media to reach voters have

made money a necessity in elections. This need for money has set two requirements of democratic elections—political equality and freedom—at odds with
each other. Governmental reaction to this dilemma—driven by the U.S. Supreme
Court's ruling in the *Buckley* case—has been to consistently give the freedom to
spend precedence over political equality. Governmental attempts at promoting
equality have been repeatedly invalidated by the courts. Moreover, the public ambivalence and lack of urgency about campaign finance helps maintain the status
quo favoring the freedom to spend.

The preference given to the freedom to spend has had serious implications for
our political system. In the next two chapters, I will show the inequalities that
arise from the U.S. system's preference for the freedom to spend and the impact
that the resultant inequalities have on our system. In Chapter 4 I will focus on the
inequalities that exist in elections. In Chapter 5 I will lay out the inequalities that
exist on the contributor side and discuss their implications.

Notes

1. For an account of early party financing around the turn of the century, see Louise
Overacker, *Money in Elections* (New York: Macmillan, 1932).

2. For more on how political-party machines operated, see Mike Royko, *Boss: Richard J.
Daley of Chicago* (New York: Dutton, 1971).

3. James K. Pollock, Jr., *Party Campaign Funds* (New York: Alfred A Knopf, 1926).

4. From a practical view, backing candidates in their own primaries could lead to divi-
siveness in the party, especially if the party supports the ultimate loser. From a legal view,
most states simply do not allow party involvement on behalf of candidates in primary elections. Some states do allow for party influence in primaries. Minnesota's parties hold
preprimary endorsing conventions that allow the parties to endorse candidates before the
primary election. Other states, like Colorado, allow the parties to control access to their
primary ballot by requiring candidates to get a certain percentage of the party's state con-
vention vote in order to be placed on the ballot.

5. See Paul Herrnson, *Party Campaigning in the 1980s* (Cambridge, Mass.: Harvard University Press, 1988); Anthony Gierzynski, *Legislative Party Campaign Committees in the
American States* (Lexington: University Press of Kentucky, 1992).

6. Anthony Corrado, "A History of Federal Campaign Finance Law: Introduction," in
Anthony Corrado, Thomas E. Mann, Daniel R. Ortiz, Trevor Potter, and Frank J. Sorauf,
editors, *Campaign Finance Reform: A Sourcebook* (Washington, D.C.: Brookings, 1997).

7. Corrado., "A History of Federal Campaign Finance Law."

8. Frank J. Sorauf, *Money in American Elections* (Glenview, Ill.: Scott, Foresman, 1988).

9. 424 U.S. 1.

10. 435 U.S. 765.

11. 116 S. Ct. 2309 (1996).

12. Linda Greenhouse, "Justices Reject Appeals in Two Cases Involving Limits on Political Money," *The New York Times*, November 17, 1998, A18.

13. Ibid.

14. Michael J. Malbin and Thomas L. Gais, *The Day After Reform: Sobering Campaign Finance Lessons from the American States* (Albany, N.Y.: The Rockefeller Institute Press, 1998).

15. Anthony Corrado, "Party Soft Money," in Corrado et al., editors, *Campaign Finance Reform: A Sourcebook*.

16. Federal Election Commission, "FEC Reports Major Increase in Party Activity for 1995–96," (Washington, D.C.: FEC Press Release, 1997).

17. David Magleby and Marianne Holt, "The Long Shadow of Soft Money and Issue-Advocacy Ads," *Campaigns and Elections*, May 1999, volume 20, no. 4, 22–27.

18. Malbin and Gais, *The Day After Reform*.

19. Deborah Beck, Paul Taylor, Jeffrey Stanger, and Douglas Rivlin, *Issue Advocacy During the 1996 Campaign: A Catalog* (Philadelphia: Annenberg Public Policy Center of the University of Pennsylvania, 1997).

20. The Annenberg Public Policy Center of the University of Pennsylvania, "Issue Ad Spending (1997–1998)," http://appcpenn.org/issueads/estimate.htm.

21. EMILY is an acronym for "Early Money Is Like Yeast" and is intended to stress the importance of startup funds for female candidates.

22. Anthony Corrado, *Creative Campaigning: PACs and the Presidential Selection Process* (Boulder, Colo.: Westview Press, 1992).

23. Malbin and Gais, *The Day After Reform*, 13.

24. Corrado and Ortiz, "Recent Innovations."

25. James Lewis, Anthony Gierzynski, and Paul Kleppner, *Equality of Opportunity? Financing the 1991 Campaigns for Chicago City Council* (Chicago: Chicago Urban League, 1995).

26. Corrado and Ortiz, "Recent Innovations."

27. Rating campaign-finance laws is not a simple task. One has to take into account a variety of possible restrictions and limitations. I have focused on contribution limits, prohibitions on direct contributions from corporations and labor unions, expenditure limits, and the scope of public financing. The specifics of the scoring were as follows: states with no limits on contributions or prohibitions on corporations or labor unions were scored a "1." States with some limits on contributions but no prohibition on corporate and/or labor contributions were scored a "2." State with relatively tight limits on contributions and prohibitions or strict limits on corporate and labor contributions were scored a "3." Partial public funding with corresponding limits on expenditures as well as contributions were scored a "4." And full public funding or partial public funding that applied to a wide number of state offices was scored a "5."

28. It is scored a "2" despite the bans on direct corporate and labor contributions because these types of contributors are still free to play a role in federal elections; they can make soft-money contributions.

29. Malbin and Gais, *The Day After Reform*.

30. Herbert McClosky and John Zaller, *The American Ethos: Public Attitudes Toward Capitalism and Democracy* (Cambridge, Mass.: Harvard University Press); Stanely Feldman, "Structure and Consistency in Public Opinion: the Role of Core Beliefs and Values," *American Journal of Political Science* 32 (1988), 416–440.

31. One survey found that 95 percent of respondents agreed with the statement, "Every citizen should have an equal chance to influence government policy." (James W. Prothro and Charles Grigg, "Fundamental Principles of Democracy: Bases of Agreement and Disagreement," *Journal of Politics* 22 (May 1960), 276–294.)

32. Princeton Survey Research Associates for The Pew Charitable Trust and the Center for Responsive Politics, *Money and Politics Survey,* conducted April 1–24, 1997, on a sample of 1,404 adults, with a margin of error plus or minus three percentage points. The exact wording of the question was, "I'm going to read you some different proposals to change the way federal election campaigns are run. As I read each proposal, tell me if you would strongly favor it, somewhat favor it, somewhat oppose it, or strongly oppose it. How about this proposal, banning all private contributions and using government funds to pay for ALL congressional and presidential campaigns, which would not cost more than five dollars per person."

33. Since not everyone in the survey was asked to respond to both sets of reforms, an analysis of what percentage of respondents supported both the total public funding and the totally free system is not possible. It is possible, however, to look at a similar contradiction by looking at the overlap between those who supported a totally unlimited system and those who favored "limiting or banning contributions by political action committees." A cross-tab analysis finds that 31.3 percent of respondents favored both a totally free system and the limits or ban on PACs. That is, one third of the respondents seemed to have conflicting views about freedom and equality when it comes to campaign finance.

34. The complete wording of the question was, "Keeping in mind that many different issues compete for their attention this year, how much of a priority would you like to see the president and Congress give to reforming the campaign finance system to reduce the role of money in politics? Should it be their top priority, a high priority, a medium priority, or a low priority?"

35. The exact wording of the question was, "We'd like you to rate campaign-finance reform as a priority for the president and Congress compared with some other issues. Which should have a higher priority this year—campaign finance reform or balancing the federal budget (improving education, reforming Medicare and Social Security, reducing crime and violence, opening up foreign markets for U.S. goods)?"

4

Money in Elections

Above everything, *the people are powerless if the political
enterprise is not competitive.* It is the competition of
political organizations that provides the people with the
opportunity to make a choice. Without this opportunity
popular sovereignty amounts to nothing.[1]

—E. E. Schattschneider

IF YOU WERE HOLDING a debate between two candidates, would you think it fair if one side were allotted thirty minutes to make its case and the other side only one minute? Would the audience of such a debate be able to make a rational and informed decision as to which side had more merit? Or would it be fair if the sides had thirty and ten minutes, respectively? What about thirty and twenty minutes each? Since money in campaigns buys time with the voters, such questions are the issue facing us with the financing of political campaigns. If the contribution of different sides to the discourse in a political campaign is lopsided, and if other sources of information are limited, then the information voters have about the issues will be dominated by the side that has more money to spend.

Money *does not* buy elections. Nor is money always the most important factor in determining the outcome of elections. But in these days of separately run, media-intensive campaigns, money is important. Campaigns need it to communicate with voters and compete. Because money is related to a campaign's ability to compete, the distribution of money among campaigns is important to the functioning of our elections. This is most obvious in the extreme case, when a candidate does not have sufficient money to compete (and such cases are real, not hypothetical, in U.S. elections). When that happens, elections lack competition. And elections without competition deprive voters of a meaningful choice and thus fail to function as mechanisms of popular control of government. It is also true in the less extreme case, namely when one candidate (or set of candidates or group) has a significant financial advantage. That financial advantage is an electoral advantage if it is used to effectively communicate more messages more often to voters. In such a case voters are deprived of balanced and sufficient information for their choice, weakening elections as a mechanism of popular control.

The purpose of this chapter is to look for financial inequalities among candidates, political parties, and ballot measure campaigns that are caused by our system's bias toward the freedom to spend. Given the discussion in previous chapters, we should expect to find some disparities. Before looking for disparities in campaign money, though, it is important to first see how money affects election outcomes, for the financial disparities among campaigns are only important if the things that money buys affect voters' decisions.

Money and Election Returns

The role of money in elections is much like the role of money in major-league baseball. In baseball, money is necessary to buy enough talent in order to field a reasonably competitive team. It takes even more money to build a team that can win consistently. Teams with roughly equal payrolls compete on a relatively equal field, leaving the outcome of the game to other factors. Teams with significantly larger payrolls can lose any game to teams with lesser payrolls, but over the long haul of the season, the team that spent more and thus has more talent will win more ball games. This is why many involved with baseball are concerned about financial inequalities among teams. (In fact, Major League Baseball has created a blue-ribbon panel to discuss the disparities in revenues among teams. Included on this panel are the former Senate majority leader, George Mitchell, the former chairman of the Federal Reserve Board, Paul Volcker, and the political columnist George Will (who is also a part owner of the Baltimore Orioles.)[2] Teams in major markets that earn a lot of money, like the New York Yankees and Atlanta Braves, end up with a payroll, and ultimately talent advantage, and consequently win more often. Teams that spend the least, according to *USA Today's* analysis, are taken "out of contention."[3] The failure of the Chicago Cubs—a team in a major market with a very lucrative media arrangement—to win a World Series since 1908 (or even a pennant since 1945) just shows that having money, while important, isn't everything. It can be spent poorly, or it may be that there are factors that just keep some teams from winning (like the "billy goat" curse).[4]

In most elections, money is necessary to compete, and the more money campaigns have, the better they can compete. Campaigns with a significant financial advantage are, on the average, much more likely to win. An underfunded campaign can, on occasion, defeat its highly funded opposition, but, across all elections, the candidates with more money fare much better than those with less. Conversely, some extremely well funded campaigns have lost (the Democratic primary for governor in California is the most recent example).[5] Underfunded candidates win, and candidates with a significant financial advantage lose because money, while a necessity, isn't all there is to winning elections. There are many other factors that affect the outcome of elections such as the candidates' overall appeal, the experience and celebrity of the candidates, the political loyalties of the electorate, whether the candidate is an incumbent, the state of the economy, the appeal of the candidates at the top of the ballot, and so on. To put it another way, money is a necessary ingredient for winning elections, but it is not the only ingredient.

In order to assess the impact of campaign money on electoral outcomes, political scientists have developed models of elections that include many of the various factors that affect the vote aside from candidates' campaign spending. These complex models allow us to measure the impact of campaign spending on candidates' votes while controlling for the impact of other factors. The models take the form of equations that run something along the lines of the following:

candidates' vote percentage = baseline vote for that type of candidate
                                        + candidates' spending
                                        + opponents' spending
                                        + the quality/experience of the candidate
                                        + the political party of the candidate
                                        + the partisanship of the electorate
                                        + incumbency status of the candidate

It may be easier to understand this point visually, so a graphic depiction of these sort of equations is presented in Figure 4.1. Running such models statistically, political scientists have found that money is a significant and often important factor related to candidate vote shares in U.S. Senate elections,[6] U.S. House elections,[7] gubernatorial contests,[8] state legislative primaries,[9] state legislative general elections,[10] and city council elections.[11] Additionally, it is clear that money plays a very important role in presidential nomination contests.[12] There have now been numerous empirical/scientific studies of elections that have found a relationship between the amount of money a candidate spends and his or her share of the vote across many different electoral settings in the United States. The number and consistency of the findings of these studies gives us a high level of confidence that campaign money does indeed play an important role in elections.[13]

The importance of money in campaigns, however, isn't the same for all election contests. As I pointed out in Chapter 1, when candidates can reach a large portion of the voters directly—as is the case in New Hampshire State House races— money will likely be relatively unimportant. When there are too many voters to reach directly, the need for a way to contact a lot of voters at once—via mass media—makes money important. As I suggested by the theory in Chapter 2, there are other conditions of elections that make money more or less important. Generally, spending by open-seat candidates and challengers is more important than spending by incumbents. Open-seat candidates and challengers need money in order to make them known and then to compare themselves with their opponents. Incumbents are usually relatively well known, so they need money mainly to respond to challenges from their opponents.

The effect of campaign spending also seems to follow the principle of diminishing marginal returns. That is, as spending by candidates increases their share of

FIGURE 4.1   Election model: factors that affect candidates' vote shares

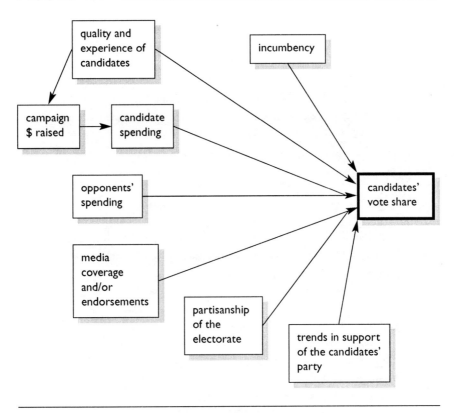

the vote does not increase at the same rate. Instead, it appears that the initial spending by campaigns is strongly related to the percent of the vote won, but as candidates spend more, the additional spending is associated with smaller increases in the vote than initial spending. For example, the first $10,000 spent is associated with a greater gain in votes than the tenth $10,000 spent (see Figure 4.1 for a graphic depiction of this relationship). The diminishing returns of spending makes sense if you consider that the initial spending by candidates is for something simple—namely, getting the candidate known (familiarity with a candidate's name alone has been shown to increase voters propensity to vote for that candidate). After gaining name recognition, the task of persuading voters becomes more difficult. Candidates must communicate with hard-to-reach voters and transmit more information more often. So the return on spending for these purposes is lower than the return on the basic levels of spending. This doesn't mean their spending becomes ineffective—it just takes bigger increases in spending to get the same effect.

To give you a sense of the nature of the impact of money, I will discuss the results of study that David Breaux and I did on state legislative elections in twelve states.[14] We developed a model of state legislative elections and ran the models for incumbent candidates, challengers, and open-seat candidates of both parties along the lines of the model in Figure 4.1. (For the details regarding this analysis, see Appendix A.) The results are in Figure 4.2. The figure shows how Democratic open-seat candidates' vote percent (the y axis) increases as candidate spending increases (the x axis[15]).

From this graph you should be able to see how the spending of the first $10,000 brings state legislative challengers up to competitiveness quickly. Following that, additional spending by the candidates increases their vote, but at a much slower rate. The point at which the return from money spent begins to diminish depends upon the election. In elections with more people to reach, the level at which candidates are brought up to competitiveness will be higher. William Cassie and David Breaux demonstrated this by estimating the dollar threshold for competitiveness in state-house contests. For California Assembly races (with district populations of 375,000) the threshold was about $100,000, while the threshold for state house races in Maine (with district populations of 8,200) was $1,000.[16]

In addition to candidate campaign spending, there are a lot of other expenditures being made in an attempt to affect election outcomes these days. There are independent expenditures and issue-advocacy expenditures by interest groups and political parties, and there is spending in campaigns for or against voter initiatives and referendums. While little research has been carried out to measure the impact of independent and issue-advocacy spending, it is reasonable to suspect that spending in these cases matters much in the same way that it does with candidates' spending. Anecdotally, President Clinton attributed his rise in popularity in 1995 (which helped him get reelected) to issue ads run by the DNC (the same ad campaign that was the source of the questionable fund-raising practices detailed in Chapter 1).

With regard to voter initiatives and referenda, money clearly plays an important role. Large sums of money are needed just to collect enough signatures to get an initiative on the ballot. By way of illustration, the Center for Responsive Politics estimates that the drive to get enough signatures to qualify the ten measures on the Oregon ballot for 1998 cost sponsors $2 million.[17] In fact, companies that specialize in collecting signatures for ballot questions have become a big busi-

FIGURE 4.2   **Relationship between spending and the vote for Democratic open-seat candidates in state house elections in twelve states (CA, CO, IA, IN, KY, MI, MN, MO, NY, OR, WA, WI)**

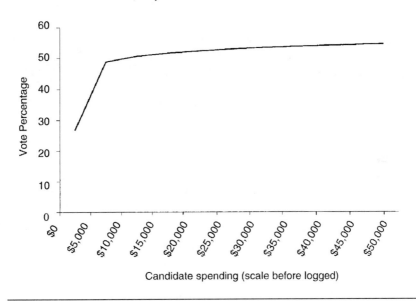

Candidate spending (scale before logged)

Source: Created by author from previously published results.

ness.[18] Spending in efforts in support of or in opposition to ballot questions is likely to be effective since voters usually have little knowledge of the ballot questions and tend to make up their mind in the last two weeks before the election.[19] Additionally, ballot questions are different from choosing candidates. When choosing candidates, voters can simplify their decision by basing their vote on their political predispositions toward a political party or toward the incumbent (a candidate's party is usually on the ballot, and most voters know the incumbent). The lack of such voting cues and predispositions on ballot questions makes the voters more susceptible to persuasive messages about the ballot issue. These suspicions are backed up by analyses of ballot elections that have found that campaign money does play a very important role in the success or failure of ballot measures.[20]

In summary, campaign spending in elections is an important factor in election outcomes. This correlation has been empirically verified repeatedly and in different types of elections. How important money actually is does vary across electoral contexts and settings in the United States—start-up levels of spending are much more important than later expenditures, and spending is more important for nonincumbent candidates than for incumbents. But the main point here is that money does play a role in election outcomes—not the simple "buying of elections" many would believe, but an important role nonetheless. Because money is important in elections, the distribution of money in elections becomes important, and inequalities among candidates have implications for the democratic nature of our elections.

The Distribution of Money

Since money does play an important role in elections, the distribution of money in electoral systems is important. If the distribution of money among campaigns is random, inequities in that distribution of money would not pose a great problem for our elections. But, as extensive literature in political science shows (and as I will illustrate in this section), the distribution of money in campaigns is not random but instead follows general patterns. And these patterns of the distribution of money have implications for how well elections function and how well, in turn, equal political representation is achieved in the U.S. political system.

Two premises that I have discussed to this point should lead us to believe that the distribution of money in elections is unequal. The first premise is that those who have money to contribute in significant amounts to elections often have common interests in governmental policy. The second premise is that money in politics flows to the points of power, to those in the political system who have influence over the direction that government takes. If these premises are correct, money should flow to those in a position of power who are most likely to support the interests of those who contribute. In the American pluralist system, power over government policy is located in many different places, including incumbent law makers, legislative committees, committee chairs, party leaders, and incumbent parties. This arrangement should lead us to expect to find that powerful incumbents—committee chairs, party leaders—and Republican parties would accrue a significant advantage in raising money in our political system. Those who do not have sufficient power to attract campaign contributions have an alternative: their own wealth. This route, however, is obviously limited to a few individuals, making it difficult for candidates of lesser means to break into the system.

The Incumbency Advantage

The incumbency advantage in fund-raising is extremely well documented in the political science literature. According to Paul Herrnson, the "typical House incumbent involved in a two-party contest raised just under $750,000 in cash and party coordinated expenditures in 1996, which is over two and one-half times more than the typical House challenger. . . . The typical Senate incumbent raised about $1.5 million more than the typical challenger during the 1996 election."[21] While some may argue that the gap is due to the fact that there are many challengers who are just not high-quality challengers, the gap between competitive challengers and incumbents is still very large. Herrnson calculates that incumbents in competitive races (with margins of 20 percent or less of the vote) "raised over 65 percent more in cash and party coordinated expenditures than did hopeful challengers during the 1996 elections."[22]

The gap between incumbents and challengers in congressional races increased dramatically from the late 1970s to 1992 (see figure 4.3). Challenger spending over that period went from about two-thirds of incumbent spending to one-third of incumbent spending in House races. The 1994 and 1996 elections witnessed a slight increase in the relative spending of challengers in House races, but their spending remained under one-half that of incumbents. In the 1998 election challengers' disadvantage increased again, their spending dropping down to 27 percent of that of incumbents.

The gap between Senate challengers and Senate incumbents also increased between 1980 and 1992. In 1994, however, the gap decreased dramatically, with challengers raising close to 90 percent of what incumbents raised. In 1996 and 1998 challengers lost ground again, though they stayed closer to the incumbents' fund-raising than challengers did from 1984 to 1992. The dramatic improvement for challengers in 1994 (as well as the decent showing in 1996 and 1998) is due largely to a substantial increase in the amounts of their own money that candidates sank into their campaigns (in cash and in personal loans). Candidate contributions to their campaigns constituted 3 percent of the funds raised by Democratic challengers and 17 percent of the revenues raised by Republican challengers in 1992. In 1994, 24 percent of Democratic challengers' revenues and 44 percent of Republican challengers' revenues came from their own checkbooks.[23] For the 1996 election Democratic challengers' percent of revenue coming from their own pockets increased again to 37 percent, whereas Republicans' dropped down to 3 percent. For the 1998 election about 30 percent of both Democratic and Republican challengers' revenues came from the candidates' own pocket. Apparently, one

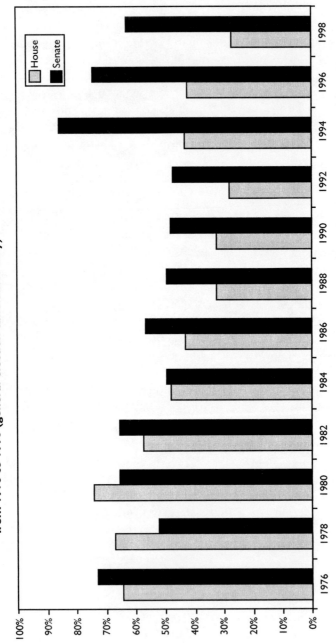

FIGURE 4.3   **Challenger spending as a percentage of incumbent spending for U.S. House and Senate races from 1976 to 1996 (general-election candidates only)**

Source: Produced by author from data presented in Norman J. Ornstein, Thomas E. Mann, and Michael J. Malbin, *Vital Statistics on Congress, 1997–1998* (Washington, D.C.: Congressional Quarterly Press, 1998), and the Federal Election Commission, http://www.fec.gov/press/sgnlng98.htm, http://www.fec.gov/press/hgnlng98.htm.

way to overcome incumbents' advantage in fund-raising is to pay your own way, an option not open to most people.

The incumbency advantage in campaign money is found in state and local contests as well. Gary Moncrief's analysis of median expenditures of incumbents and challengers in state house races in eighteen states in 1992 found that median challenger spending was below 50 percent of median incumbent spending in twelve of the states.[24] And, as suggested previously, the gap between challenger spending and incumbent spending was the widest in states that tend to have more expensive campaigns (see Figure 4.4; the states are arranged in groups going from most expensive campaigns to least expensive). These more expensive campaigns tend to be in larger districts that, because of the size of the task of contacting voters, make spending substantial sums of money a necessity. Thus, in the places where money is more important, the gap between challengers and incumbents is greater and therefore more damaging.

The reader should note that despite being at the higher end of the spending scale, Wisconsin and Minnesota do not exhibit as great a gap between challenger spending and incumbent spending. These states are the only two states in the group that provided public funds to candidates in state legislative races. The public funds clearly allowed challengers to narrow the gap with incumbents in terms of spending in these states.

Additionally, Moncrief's analysis of challenger and incumbent spending over time led him to conclude that "the relative position of challengers is not improving in most states," and is in fact declining is some.[25] The case of California—one of the "freest" campaign-finance systems—illustrates the increasing disadvantage challengers face. Figure 4.5 traces the incumbency advantage for California State Assembly races from 1976 to 1996.

The advantage incumbents have over challengers is even greater in state legislative primaries. David Breaux and I (in an analysis of primaries for the state house in six states over a number of election cycles) found that the ratio of the average incumbent's revenue to the average challenger's revenue in contested races was greater than three to one in all but two of twenty cases.[26] Incumbent candidates in contested primaries in Illinois in 1988, for example, raised, on average, five and a half times more money than challengers. From our analysis it appears that much of incumbents' advantage in fund-raising comes early on. Incumbents carry over substantial amounts of money from their previous campaigns, and they raise substantially more prior to the primary election. Challengers fare better during the general election season but not enough to come close to what incumbents raise.[27]

Information on the financing of city elections is hard to come by, but one study of Chicago city-council elections found major disparities between incumbents

FIGURE 4.4   **Challengers' spending (median) as a percentage of incumbent expenditures (median) in contested state house races**

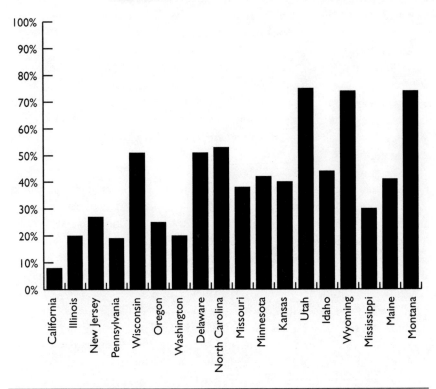

Source: Developed by the author from data published in Gary F. Moncrief, "Candidate Spending in State Legislative Races," in Joel A. Thompson and Gary F. Moncrief, *Campaign Finance in State Legislative Elections* (Washington, D.C.: Congressional Quarterly Press, 1998).

and challengers. In the 1995 aldermanic races the average incumbent spent $89,963, whereas the average challenger spent $20,751. On the revenue side, incumbents averaged $141,538 in revenues raised compared with the challengers' $29,734.[28]

The evidence is quite unequivocal: there is a substantial amount of inequality when it comes to the financial resources of incumbents and challengers in legislative contests. The interaction between this financial advantage and the advantage that incumbents accrue from their office—greater media visibility and name

FIGURE 4.5   **Median expenditures for incumbents and challengers in California State Assembly races, 1976 to 1996**

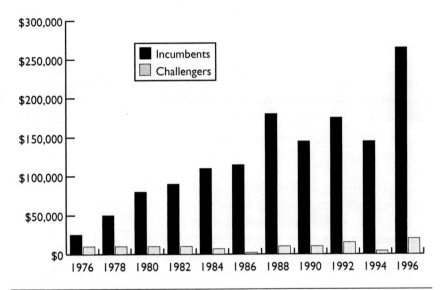

Source: Produced by author from data made available from the California Secretary of State, http://www.ss.ca.gov/prd/finance96/table6.htm.

recognition, the franking privilege, the ability to use their office to provide service and bring home money to the district—make it very difficult to defeat an incumbent. Between 1986 to 1996, incumbent U.S. Representatives who ran for reelection were reelected at an average rate 94 percent.[29] The success rates for state legislative incumbents are equally high, with better than 90 percent of incumbents winning reelection in most states.[30] And, in an upward spiral of cause and effect, incumbency is self-perpetuating: because incumbents are more successful, they tend to attract more money, as they attract more money, they are more difficult to defeat, and so on.

The evident inequality between incumbents and challengers interferes with the functioning of elections as means for popular control of government, which reduces political equality. The disparities in campaign finance between incumbents and challengers helps to make many legislative elections uncompetitive. Indeed, the size of the margins by which incumbents win has increased in both national and state elections, as has the number of races without any competition.[31] The lack of competition deprives the electorate of a choice at the polls. Without meaningful choices many potential voters become disillusioned and choose to stay home on election day, losing their voice in governance. In addition to providing choices with regard to governance, elections are also supposed to make elected officials more responsive to the public. Electoral competition, it is believed, fosters responsiveness. The imbalance in campaign money reduces competition and therefore reduces elections as a means of making officials more responsive to the public. So candidates have a great deal of freedom to raise and spend money while political equality is eroded by the lack of meaningful choices in elections and the lack of responsiveness that follows. Under these conditions elections malfunction. They allow for a lot of freedom but fail to act as a vehicle for equal political representation.

A note about term limits. Limiting the number of terms that legislators can serve has been promoted as one way to reduce the power of incumbents and increase competition in elections. I believe that term limits will fail to increase competition. Instead, term limits will just regularize competition. Legislative seats will be competitive every *x* number of years when the incumbent is forced from office by the term limit. In between the terms competition will decrease since potential candidates, who know it is more difficult to run against an incumbent, will simply wait until the incumbent is forced from office by term limits. Additionally, term limits have other unintended consequences, such as weakening the legislative body vis-à-vis the executive branch, legislative staff, and interest groups by depriving the legislative institution of institutional memory and expertise needed to effectively carry out their constitutional duties. Term limits are a quick and simple idea that will not restore political equality via electoral competition to the institution of elections—only changes in how the United States finances its campaigns will do that.

Political-Party Financing

Inequality between the Democratic and Republican parties could be more harmful than inequalities between incumbent candidates and their challengers. It could be more harmful because despite common rhetoric, these political parties do represent different views of the proper role and scope of government. Incumbents, being from both parties, do not. The two major American parties are not as different as parties in many European systems, but government policy does differ in important ways, depending on which party is in control. It differs enough that business interests and the interest of those at the higher end of the income scale tend to ally themselves with the Republican party. This confluence of political in-

• •

**FIGURE 4.6   Flow of money by party
control of government**

When Democrats control the government:

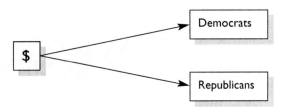

When Republicans control the government:

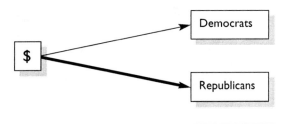

terest and wealth in our society should lead us to suspect that the Republican party has an advantage over the Democrats in the area of campaign finance. This advantage is conditioned, however, by which party is in power. If the Democrats are in power, then moneyed interests will seek to secure access to Democrats through campaign contributions because Democrats then have the power to affect those interests. In such a situation, the Republicans' advantage in fund-raising would be reduced.

In Figure 4.7, I present a comparison of the revenues (hard money only) of the Democratic and Republican national committees since the 1977–78 election cycle (the numbers include money raised by the congressional campaign committees as well as the national committees). Clearly, the Republican committees have consistently had a significant advantage over the Democratic committees in raising revenue over the years. In one election cycle (1981–82) the Republicans had five times the amount available to the Democratic committees. In the 1995–96 cycle—the one in which Democratic fund-raising practices came under fire—the

FIGURE 4.7 Federal revenues (hard money) raised by Democratic and Republican party committees, 1977–1998

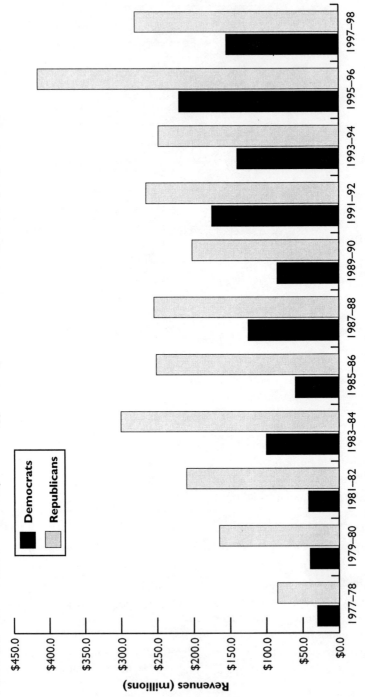

Source: Created by the author from data published by the Federal Election Committee, http://www.fec.gov/press/ptyye98.htm.

Democrats managed to raise only half as much as the Republicans. Figure 4.7 doesn't, however, tell the entire story because the chart doesn't include soft money, that money raised outside of the federal regulatory regime for the purpose of general party activity.

In Figure 4.8 I present the amounts of soft money raised by the two major parties over the last four election cycles. From this chart one can see that Democrats do not catch up to Republicans by raising more soft money—Republicans also raise more soft money than do Democrats, though by a smaller margin between 1991 and 1996. Republicans had a significant advantage in soft money in the 1998 election.

It is clear from these data that the Republican national committees have a significant edge over the Democrats in fund-raising. In this light the frantic and often questionable Democratic fund-raising led by President Clinton can be seen as understandable if not excusable. The unequal abilities of the parties to raise money drove the Democrats to raise as much money as possible so as not to be outgunned by the Republicans.

It should be noted that the amount of money raised by the political parties is not merely a reflection of the popular support of each of the parties. More people have identified themselves as Democrats than Republicans in polls since the New Deal realignment. In 1996, 39 percent of the public considered themselves Democrats, and 29 percent considered themselves Republicans.[32] The inequality of financial resources between the parties is instead a reflection of the wealth of those who tend to support the Republican party. As shown in Figure 4.9, more people with higher family incomes tend to identify with the Republican party than the Democratic party. The higher the level of income, the more people identify with the Republicans and the more money individuals have to contribute to political parties or campaigns. Research on campaign contributors confirms this trend. In a study of various forms of participation, Verba, Schlozman, and Brady found that the most important determinant of the extent of campaign contributions is family income. "To give money one needs money and, apparently, little else." [33] Another study found that 81 percent of contributors to congressional campaigns had family incomes above $100,000.[34] Only 5 percent of contributions came from those making less than $50,000. These wealthy contributors were more likely to identify themselves as conservative Republicans than any other category, and tended to be conservative on economic matters.[35]

In addition to the upper-income and conservative bias of individual contributors, contributions from the corporate sector also tend to favor Republicans. Business PACs are by far the largest group of PAC contributors, having contributed more than $147 million to candidates in the 1995–96 election cycle (compare that to the next closest group of PACs, labor, which contributed $49 million).[36] Some

FIGURE 4.8   **National party nonfederal (soft) money raised, 1991–1998**

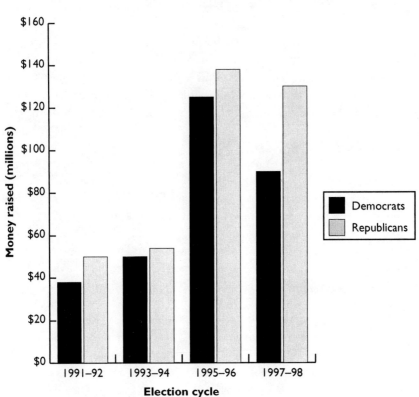

Source: Created by the author from data published by the Federal Election Committee, http://www.fec.gov/press/ptyye98.htm.

70 percent of their contributions went to Republican candidates! Corporations were also the dominant source of soft money contributions (88 percent of soft money came from corporations); 54 percent of that money went to Republicans in 1996.[37]

So the confluence of wealth and conservatism on economic issues leads to a large advantage in resources for Republicans at the national level. Additionally, some have argued that the need to raise money from higher-income, more conservative citizens and businesses has forced the Democratic party to be more conservative than it would otherwise be. That is, in order to raise enough money to

• •

FIGURE 4.9   **Percentage identifying with the Democratic and Republican parties by family income level, 1996**

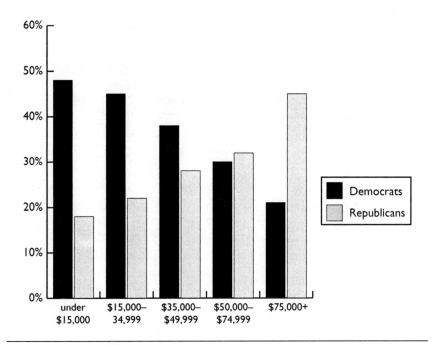

Source: 1996 American National Election Study.

compete, Democrats have had to move to the right on economic policy.[38] There still are differences between the parties on economic policy priorities—witness the government shutdown in 1995—largely because the Republicans have shifted even farther to the right. Nonetheless, the Democrats appear to have abandoned their tradition of promoting economic equality through large governmental programs. President Clinton, a Democrat, declared in his 1995 State of the Union Address that "the era of big government is over" and signed the Personal Responsibility and Work Ethic Reconciliation Act of 1996 (which ended the federal guarantee of public assistance for the poor that had been in place since the Depression of the 1930s). Thus, representation of those who support government promotion of economic equality suffers because of the political inequality inherent in the lightly regulated private financing of our elections.

In addition to the national party committees, the political parties also have state and local committees that are financially active in elections. Does the Republican advantage at the national level hold at the state level, too? Do the Democrats make up for their disadvantage at the national level by raising more at the state level? That depends on the state. State politics is not simply national politics on a smaller scale, and state parties are more than just local branches of the national party committees. Party ideology and support for each party does vary from one state to the next. While it has been found that the Democrats in any state are always more liberal than the Republicans in the same state,[39] the Democratic party in some states may be sufficiently conservative to receive the financial support of wealthy individuals and businesses. Moreover, the strain of strong social conservatism characteristic of Republicans in some states may turn off potential wealthy contributors whose conservatism is mainly limited to economic policy.

How, in fact, do the parties compare at the state level? Ideally we would like to look at the financing for the state parties in all of the states, but data on state campaign finance are difficult to come by because each state is responsible for its own records. I have collected information on the revenues of state parties during the 1996 election cycle for several states and present them in Figure 4.10.[40]

It is clear from Figure 4.10 that Democratic state committees do not make up for the relative deficiency of their national committees. In fact, in most of the states Republican committees have the edge in financial resources. Democrats have an advantage in party funds in the low-finance state of Vermont and a very slim advantage in Virginia, where Democrats tend to be more conservative than northern Democrats. The Republicans have the edge in the rest. It is important to see whether the advantage Republicans have in these states is just a phenomenon of the 1996 election. The New Jersey data, being cumulative data over four years, already do this. I was able to obtain historical data for two states, Minnesota and Washington, and I present them in Figures 4.11 and 4.12. The edge the Republicans had in these states is apparently typical for elections going back to 1984.

Political parties are a majoritarian institution in our pluralistic political system. They strive to win elections by aggregating the preferences of citizens into majority coalitions. Our elections are structured so that the party that represents the preferences of the greatest block of citizens wins. In the process the parties promote political equality in elections through the representation of those interests and by encouraging participation. Our privately financed, free-spending system contaminates the functioning of the political parties, giving the party backed by wealthier interests a financial advantage of consequence over the other, an advantage that doesn't reflect their popular support. Under our private system of financing elections, the Republican party has turned its alliance with business in-

● ●

FIGURE 4.10   State political party committee revenue, 1996

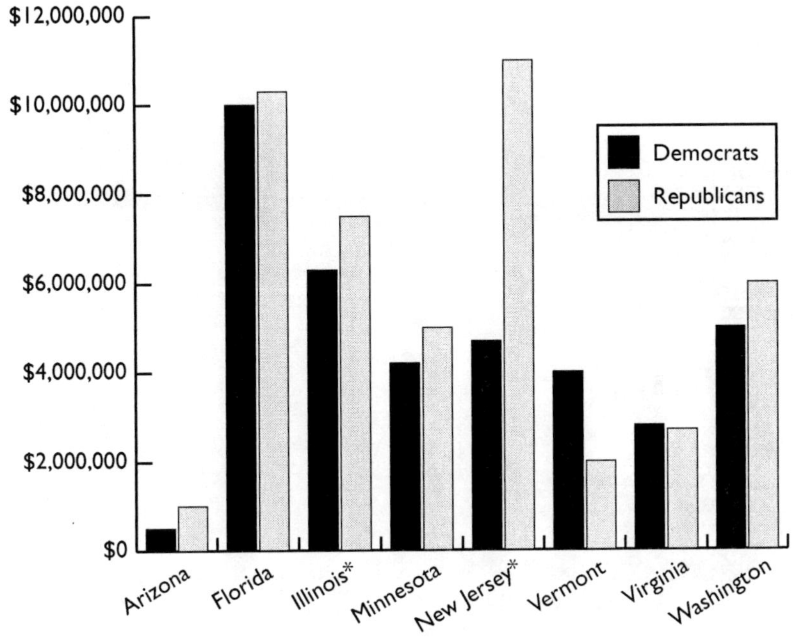

Sources: Vermont Secretary of State (photocopied reports); Virginia Public Access Project (http://www.crp.org/vpap/pac1997G.htm); Washington State Public Disclosure Commission; State of Minnesota Ethical Practices Board; "1996 Campaign Finance Reports for State Candidates, Political Committees, and Political Funds"; Center for Public Integrity, http://www.crp.org/cpi/; Center for Analysis of Public Issues, http://www.crp.org/capi; Arizona Secretary of State, http://www.sosaz.com/.
   *Illinois data are for state house and senate party campaign committees only; New Jersey data include revenues from 1993 to 1997.

terests and wealthy individuals into an advantage in campaign finance. The fact that the Democrats still control the presidency mitigates this advantage somewhat. If the Republicans ever gain both the presidency and the Congress, their financial advantage will likely increase.

Democratic Candidates vs. Republican Candidates

Do Republican candidates also have an advantage in raising revenues? Given the fact that many incumbent lawmakers in Congress and the state legislatures are

••

FIGURE 4.11   **Minnesota state political party committee revenues,
1984–1996**

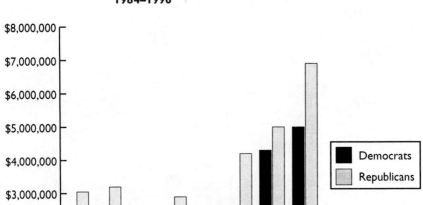

Sources: Michael J. Malbin and Thomas L. Gais, *The Day After Reform: Sobering Campaign Finance
Lessons from the American States* (Albany, N.Y.: The Rockefeller Institute Press, 1998), 125; and the
State of Minnesota Ethical Practices Board, "1996 Campaign Finance Reports for State Candidates,
Political Committees, and Political Funds."

Democrats, we might not expect to find as much of a difference in the ability of
each party's candidates to raise money. Money will flow to the points of power. So
if the chair of an important committee happens to be a Democrat, the interests
that wish to be heard in the committee deliberations will contribute to that Democrat. Figure 4.13 compares Democratic and Republican candidates for the U.S.
House and Senate for the 1998 election. Republican senatorial candidates had a
slight edge in fund-raising over their Democratic counterparts. Republican
House candidates had an even greater advantage in fund-raising.[41]

Once again, one should exercise caution in drawing conclusions from just one
year. So I charted the revenues of both parties' candidates for the Senate and
House since 1988 in Figures 4.14 and 4.15. Both charts show that the Republican

FIGURE 4.12 **Washington state political party committee revenues, 1984–1996**

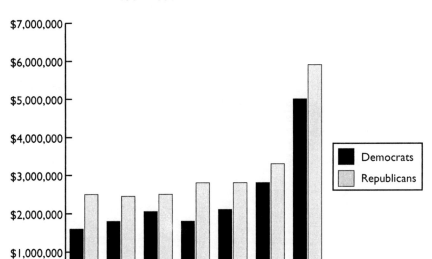

Sources: Washington State Public Disclosure Commission, *1984 (1986, 1990,* and *1996) Election Financing Fact Book;* Michael J. Malbin and Thomas L. Gais, *The Day After Reform: Sobering Campaign Finance Lessons from the American States* (Albany, N.Y.: The Rockefeller Institute Press, 1998), 119.

candidates' advantage in fund-raising isn't the same for every election. In Senate races Republicans had the advantage in four of the six election years between 1988 and 1998, with a large advantage in 1994 (the year the Republicans took control of the Senate and House).

Among House candidates, the Republicans outraised the Democrats in 1996 and 1998. The Democrats raised more money from 1988 to 1994. It wasn't until after the Republicans took control of the House in 1994 that their candidates began to raise more money than Democratic candidates did. The fact that the total amount of money raised by Republicans was less than that raised by Democrats should make one suspect that incumbency had something to do with this funding difference. Not only did the Democrats have more incumbents before 1994, but they had also been the incumbent party in the House since the 1950s. So contributors who

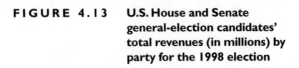

FIGURE 4.13   U.S. House and Senate
general-election candidates'
total revenues (in millions) by
party for the 1998 election

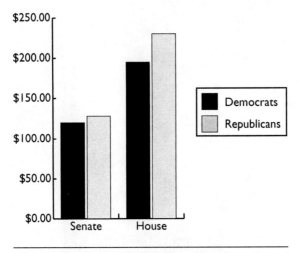

Source: Federal Election Commission, http://www.fec.gov/
finance/senlng98.htm, http://www.fec.gov/finance/hselng98t.htm.

wanted access to power had to give to incumbent Democrats. Thus a better way to compare the revenues of both parties' candidates would be to look at the average revenue for incumbents and challengers separately. I present the averages in Figure 4.16.

When average revenues for incumbents and challengers are compared, the Democratic advantage prior to 1996 disappears. The average Republican incumbent had a slight revenue advantage over the average Democratic incumbent in 1988. In 1990 and 1992 incumbents from both parties averaged roughly the same amount of revenue. Democrats had a slight edge in 1994. And Republican incumbents had a clear advantage in 1996 and 1998. Given the fact that the Democrats were in power prior to 1994, one might have thought that the average Democratic incumbent would have raised significantly more than the average Republican incumbent. The reason they did not is that, although they controlled the chamber, their politics did not fit well with that of the biggest contributors. Now that the

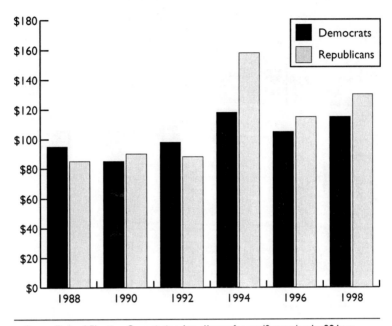

FIGURE 4.14 **U.S. Senate candidates' total revenues (in millions), 1988–1998, by political party affiliation**

Source: Federal Election Commission, http://www.fec.gov/finance/senlng98.htm.

Republicans are in control of the House, the conflict between supporting the incumbent party and ideological preference is gone for big contributors. The shift in giving among business PACs between the 1994 and 1996 election supports this point. In the 1994 election cycle Republican congressional candidates received 49 percent of business PAC dollars. In the 1996 election cycle Republican candidates received 70 percent of business PAC dollars.[42]

Republican challenger candidates do not appear, on average, to consistently be better fund-raisers than their Democratic counterparts. The average Republican challenger raised more money between 1990 and 1994. In 1996, when the Republicans focused on defending their first-term incumbents (and Democrats on challenging them), the average raised by Republican challengers dropped, while the average raised by Democratic challengers increased. In the 1998 election Republican challengers again did better than Democratic challengers.

••

FIGURE 4.15   **U.S. House candidates' total revenues
(in millions), 1988–1998, by political party
affiliation**

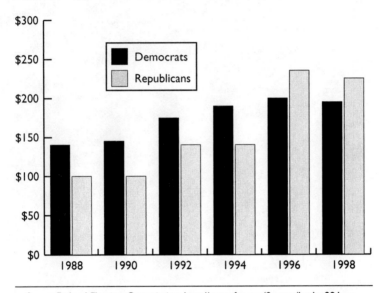

Source: Federal Election Commission, http://www.fec.gov/finance/hselng98.htm.

An examination of fund-raising by candidates at the state level reveals no consistent advantage for either party. Figure 4.17 contains the average revenues raised by all candidates in state house races for 1992 (1991 for New Jersey and Mississippi). Democratic candidates average higher revenues in nine of the seventeen states for which we have data. That average is significantly higher than Republicans in California and New Jersey. Republican candidates' average revenues are significantly higher than those of their Democratic counterparts in Oregon.

While Republican-party *organizations* have a clear advantage in fund-raising over the Democrats, Republican *candidates* do not appear to have a consistent advantage in fund-raising over Democratic candidates. Inequality among candidates appears to be more of a function of incumbency than party at this point in time. This pattern shows signs of changing at the national level, however, now that Republicans control the Congress. That control has been quickly translated into an advantage in fund-raising for Republican candidates.

• •

FIGURE 4. I 6   **Average revenue for House incumbents and challengers by party, 1988–1998 (general-election candidates only)**

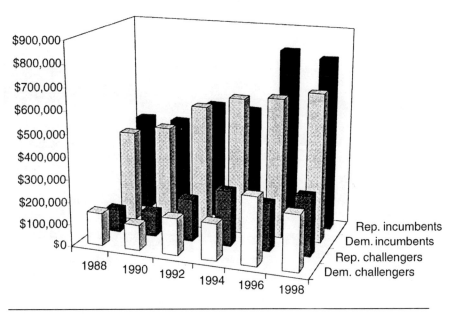

Source: Federal Election Commisiion, http://www.fec.gov/finanace/hseIng98.htm.

Initiatives and Referenda Funding

When voters enter the polling booth on election day, they will often be asked not only to choose their representatives but also to decide government policy in various areas. The procedures for putting such questions on the ballot differ from state to state (the national government has no such mechanism). Policy questions can be placed on the ballot by citizen petition, by the legislature, or automatically, as dictated by constitutional provisions. Twenty-three states allow citizens to put questions about policy matters on the ballot through either the initiative or popular referendum.[43] In 1998, an observer wrote, "In many states [voters] will face complicated and lengthy ballots on election day. . . . A total of 234 questions will appear on ballots nationwide. This number includes 61 measures initiated by citizens in the 24 initiative and referenda states, 165 measures referred by the legislatures, and 9 measures placed on the ballot by Florida's Constitution Revision Commission."[44]

84

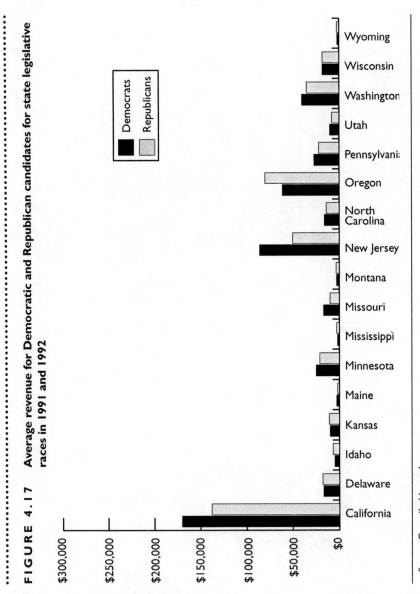

Source: Compiled by author.

FIGURE 4.17   Average revenue for Democratic and Republican candidates for state legislative races in 1991 and 1992

Democrats
Republicans

Wyoming
Wisconsin
Washington
Utah
Pennsylvania
Oregon
North Carolina
New Jersey
Montana
Missouri
Mississippi
Minnesota
Maine
Kansas
Idaho
Delaware
California

$300,000
$250,000
$200,000
$150,000
$100,000
$50,000
$0

Ballot questions put to the voters in these states covered a wide range of topics, including property-tax limits, doctor-assisted suicide, medical use of marijuana, term limits, affirmative action, abortion, campaign-finance reform, three-strike laws, riverboat gambling, gambling on Indian lands, beverage-container deposits, public services for illegal aliens, gay rights, health-care coverage, auto-insurance rates, the hunting of black bears, and so on. Almost any issue is fair game as long as the interest promoting it can gather the required number of signatures to get the question on the ballot. Once on the ballot, the policy question is decided by the voters.

Sounds very democratic, doesn't it? A chance for true political equality: voters decide, with each vote counting equally. But do initiatives and referenda live up to this promise? The flaw with this dream is that, just as in candidate elections, voters need information in order to make an informed decision on these issues. And where does that information come from? It comes from campaigns in support of or opposition to the ballot question.[45] And what do campaigns need in order to reach voters? Money, of course. A lot of money is needed just to get enough signatures to place issues on the ballot. One report, released by the Oregon Secretary of State's office, showed that "nearly $2.5 million was paid to 2,720 petition circulators to qualify initiatives for the 1996 general election."[46] Furthermore, all of the petitions that were circulated by volunteers (as opposed to paid signature gatherers) failed to make it on the ballot in 1996.

So it shouldn't be surprising that studies of the role of money in the initiative and referenda process have shown money to be a key factor in determining whether the ballot question passes.[47] If an imbalance in campaign money exists on one side of a ballot question, then the democratic nature of these exercises is put into serious doubt.

Major imbalances in the funding of these campaigns do occur, especially when the issue affects the interests of corporations. The Supreme Court, in *First National Bank of Boston et al. v. Bellotti* (435 U.S. 765, 1978) ruled that states could not limit business spending on the debate over ballot questions. The combination of this freedom to spend and the fact that these issues are decided in the election (that is, elections are the point of power) leads to a tremendous amount of spending on many of these ballot issues. Given differences in ability to spend money, very lopsided campaigns often result.

Studies of the financing of ballot measure campaigns have found major imbalances, mainly on issues involving business interests.[48] To illustrate, I charted the expenditures on a few ballot propositions involving business interests put before voters in California in 1992 and 1994 and present them in Figure 4.18. While business interests do not always win these contests (the tobacco industry lost

●●

FIGURE 4.18   **Expenditures in support of or opposition to ballot
questions involving business interests in California, 1992
and 1994**

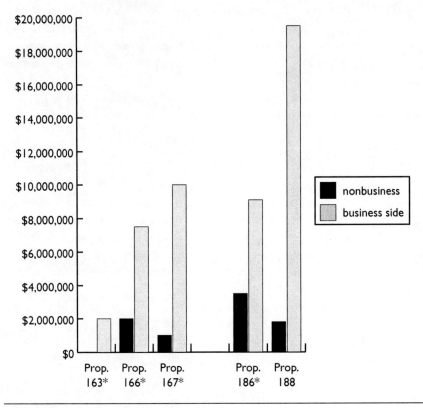

Prop. 163: ends taxation of certain food products
Prop. 166: basic health-care coverage
Prop. 167: state taxes
Prop. 186: health services, taxes
Prop. 188: preempt local tobacco laws
*Business side in ballot question won

Sources: Political Reform Division, *California's Statewide Ballot Measures: 1992 General Election Campaign* (Sacramento: California Secretary of State, 1993); Political Reform Division, *California's Statewide Ballot Measures: 1994 Primary and General Elections* (Sacramento: California Secretary of State, 1995).

Proposition 188 mainly because of media coverage of their deceptive tactics and a
subsequent voter backlash), this major inequality gives the side with money a significant advantage. As Thomas Cronin put it, "When corporations spend vast

• •

FIGURE 4.19   **Spending for and against term-limit initiatives in California (1992), Washington (1991, 1992, and 1996), Nebraska (1996), and Oregon (1996)**

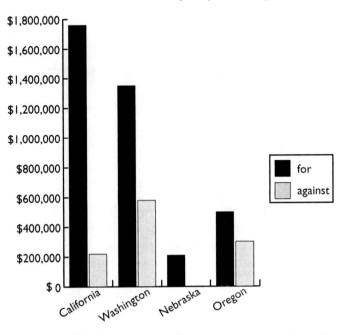

Sources: Political Reform Division, *California's Statewide Ballot Measures: 1992 General Election Campaign* (Sacramento: California Secretary of State, 1993); Washington State Public Disclosure Commission, *1996 Election Financing Fact Book;* Nebraska Accountability and Disclosure Commission, *A Summary of Political Campaign Finance: The 1996 State of Nebraska Primary and General Elections;* Oregon Secretary of State, *Summary Report of Campaign Contributions and Expenditures General Election 1996,* 1997.

sums of money to dominate discussion and debate via the media and mailbox, the voting public often hears only one side of an issue. The advantages that opposition money in large quantities can buy can rarely be overcome."[49]

Inequality in the funding of ballot issues extends beyond issues concerning business; they stem from the level of intensity and resources available to the different sides. This imbalance has prevailed in issues such as term limits. Term-limit supporters have a significant financial advantage over opponents, and the limits have passed in almost every state that allows for voter initiatives. Figure 4.19

shows the expenditures for some recent battles in California, Nebraska, Oregon, and Washington. Term-limit campaigns get support from corporate interests, the Republican party, and a national organization—U.S. Term Limits—that sinks a lot of money into these initiative campaigns. U.S. Term Limits contributed $462,235 to the Limit Congress campaign, which was organized to support Proposition 164 in California in 1992.[50]

In the initiative and referenda process the repercussions of the unlimited freedom to spend are the greatest. Lopsided campaign finances mean lopsided debate over the ballot issues. The process that promised direct democracy and political equality turns out to be one that can be controlled by the side with the financial advantage. The long-term result is a deepening of public cynicism about the political process.

Conclusion

Inequalities in a key campaign resource—money—are a major problem. A financial advantage means an advantage in the public debate that occurs during an election. It is this debate that helps many voters decide whether to vote and whom or what to vote for. In many cases the public hears the equivalent of thirty minutes of arguments for one side of the debate and two minutes for the other. News coverage, which typically focuses on the "horse race" rather than the issues of an election, does not remedy this imbalance.[51] The weakness of party affiliation among the public means that party is less of an effective voting cue for most of the population. So the imbalance between campaigns—incumbent versus challenger, Democratic party versus Republican party, and ballot supporters versus opponents—means that elections are not meeting the requirement for political equality and are consequently losing their legitimacy and importance in the eyes of the public.

Notes

1. E. E. Schattschneider, *The Semi-Sovereign People: A Realist's View of Democracy in America* (New York: Hold, Rinehart and Winston, 1960), 140.

2. Erik Brandy, "Revenue Panel Created," *USA Today*, April 2, 1999, 13C.

3. "Money Matters," *USA Today*, April 2, 1999, 13C.

4. Cub lore has it that the owner of the Billy Goat Tavern put a curse on the franchise during the 1945 World Series, when the owner of the team refused to allow the tavern owner's goat into Wrigley Field.

5. The candidate who won, Gray David, spent the least among the three major candidates. Davis spend a little under $9 million, Al Checchi spent a little under $40 million, and Jane Harman spent around $16 million (California Secretary of State, http://www.ss.ca.gov/prd/finance_98/constitutional_officers.htm).

6. Alan I. Abramowitz, "Explaining Senate Election Outcomes," *American Political Science Review* 82 (June 1988) 385–403; Charles Stewart III, "A Sequential Model of U.S. Senate Elections," *Legislative Studies Quarterly* 14 (November 1989), 567–601.

7. See Gary C. Jacobson, *Money in Congressional Elections* (New Haven: Yale University Press, 1980); Donald Philip Green and Jonathan S. Krasno, "Salvation for the Spendthrift Incumbent: Reestimating the Effects of Campaign Spending in House Elections," *American Journal of Political Science* 32 (1988), 884–907; Scott J. Thomas, "Do Incumbent Expenditures Matter?" *Journal of Politics* 51 (1989), 965–976.

8. Sarah M. Moorehouse, "Money Versus Party Effort: Nominating for Governor," *American Journal of Political Science* 34 (1990), 706–724; Samuel C. Patterson, "Campaign Spending in Contests for Governors," *Western Political Quarterly* 35 (1982), 457–477; Peverill Squire, "Challenger Profiile and Gubernatorial Elections, *Western Political Quarterly* 45 (1992), 125–142.

9. David A. Breaux and Anthony Gierzynski, "'It's Money that Matters': Campaign Expenditures in State Legislative Primaries," *Legislative Studies Quarterly* 16 (1991), 429–443.

10. See Gregory A. Caldeira and Samuel C. Patterson, "Bringing Home the Votes: Electoral Outcomes in State Legislative Races," *Political Behavior* 4 (1982), 33–67; Anthony Gierzynski and David A. Breaux, "Money and Votes in State Legislative Elections," *Legislative Studies Quarterly* 16 (1991), 203–217; Anthony Gierzynski and David A. Breaux, "Legislative Elections and the Importance of Money," *Legislative Studies Quarterly* 21 (1996), 337–357: Michael W. Giles and Anita Pritchard, "Campaign Expenditures and Legislative Elections in Florida," *Legislative Studies Quarterly* 10 (1985), 71–88; Harvey J. Tucker and Ronald E. Weber, "State Legislative Election Outcomes: Contextual Effects and Legislative Performance Effects," *Legislative Studies Quarterly* 12 (1987), 537–553; and William Welch, "The Effectiveness of Expenditures in State Legislative Races," *American Politics Quarterly* 4 (1976), 336–356.

11. Anthony Gierzynski, Paul Kleppner, and James Lewis, "Money or the Machine: Money and Votes in Chicago Aldermanic Elections," *American Politics Quarterly* 26 (1998), 160–173.

12. Clifford W. Brown, Jr., Lynda W. Powell, and Clyde Wilcox, *Serious Money: Fundraising and Contributing in Presidential Nomination Campaigns* (New York: Cambridge University Press, 1995).

13. While political-science research consistently finds a relationship between money and vote shares, we must be careful in claiming that money causes a higher vote. One possibility that is often raised is that candidates who are likely to win are also more likely to attract money for their campaign. So the question becomes, Is it the money, or was it a strong candidacy in the first place? This question has been answered by models of elections that either statistically eliminate the effect of this factor or include a control for the

strength of the candidates. At this point in time, the tests of the role of spending in elections has eliminated many of the alternative explanations for the association between money and votes, so we can now be pretty certain that there is a causal relationship.

14. See Anthony Gierzynski and David A. Breaux, "Legislative Elections and the Importance of Money," *Legislative Studies Quarterly* for more details on the model, data, and methodology.

15. The table is labeled with dollar amounts instead of the log of those amounts—as run in the model—for ease of interpretation

16. William E. Cassie and David A. Breaux, "Expenditures and Election Results," in Joel A. Thompson and Gary F. Moncrief, *Campaign Finance in State Legislative Elections* (Washington, D.C.: Congressional Quarterly Press, 1998).

17. Marian Currinder, "Losing the Initiative," *Capital Eye: A Close-up Look at Money in Politics*, September 15, 1998, 2–3.

18. Alan Rosenthal, *The Decline of Representative Democracy* (Washington, D.C.: Congressional Quarterly Press, 1998).

19. Thomas E. Cronin, *Direct Democracy* (Cambridge, Mass.: Harvard University Press, 1989).

20. John S. Shockley, *The Initiative Process in Colorado Politics: An Assessment* (Boulder: Bureau of Governmental Research and Service, University of Colorado, 1980); Steven D. Lydenberg, *Bankrolling Ballots, Update 1980: The Role of Business in Financing Ballot Question Campaigns* (New York: Council on Economic Priorities, 1981); Daniel H. Lowenstein, "Campaign Spending and Ballot Propositions: Recent Experience, Public Choice Theory, and the First Amendment," *UCLA Law Review* 29 (February 1982); Betty H. Zisk, *Money, Media, and the Grass Roots: State Ballot Issues and the Electoral Process* (Newbury Park, Calif.: Sage Publications, 1987); Shaun Bowler, Todd Donovan, and Trudi Happ, "Ballot Propositions and Information Costs: Direct Democracy and the Fatigued Voter," *Western Political Quarterly* 45 (1992), 559–568; Thomas E. Cronin, *Direct Democracy* (Cambridge: Harvard University Press, 1989); David Magelby, *Direct Legislation* (Baltimore: Johns Hopkins Press, 1984).

21. Paul S. Herrnson, *Congressional Elections: Campaigning at Home and in Washington* (Washington, D.C.: Congressional Quarterly Press, 1998), 129–131.

22. Paul S. Herrnson, *Congressional Elections: Campaigning at Home and in Washington*, 130.

23. Federal Election Commission, http://www.fec.gov/press/sgnlng98.htm.

24. Gary F. Moncrief, "Candidate Spending in State Legislative Races," in Joel A. Thompson and Gary F. Moncrief, *Campaign Finance in State Legislative Elections* (Washington, D.C.: Congressional Quarterly Press, 1998).

25. Moncrief, "Candidate Spending in State Legislative Races," 55.

26. David A. Breaux and Anthony Gierzynski, "Candidate Revenues and Expenditures in State Legislative Primaries," in Joel A. Thompson and Gary F. Moncrief, *Campaign Finance in State Legislative Elections*.

27. Breaux and Gierzynski, "'It's Money that Matters.'"

28. Anthony Gierzynski, Paul Kleppner, and James Lewis, "The Price of Democracy: Financing Chicago's 1995 City Elections" (Chicago: Private Money in Local Elections, 1996).

29. Norman J. Ornstein, Thomas E. Mann, and Michael J. Malbin, *Vital Statistics on Congress, 1997–1998* (Washington, D.C.: American Enterprise Institute for Public Policy Research).

30. David A. Breaux and Anthony Gierzynski, "Running for Reelection in American State Legislatures," in Jack R. Van Der Slik, editor, *Politics in the American States and Communities: A Contemporary Reader* (Boston: Allyn and Bacon, 1996), 97–104.

31. Breaux and Gierzynski, "Running for Reelection in American State Legislatures"; James C. Garand, "Electoral marginality in State Legislative Elections, 1968–86," *Legislative Studies Quarterly* 16 (February 1991), 7–28; Donald A. Gross and James C. Garand, "The Vanishing Marginals, 1824–1980," *Journal of Politics* 46 (1984), 224–227.

32. William H. Flanigan and Nancy H. Zingale, *Political Behavior of the American Electorate,* ninth edition, (Washington, D.C.: Congressional Quarterly Press, 1998), 62.

33. Sidney Verba, Kay Lehman Schlozman, and Henry E. Brady, *Voice and Equality: Civic Voluntarism in American Politics* (Cambridge, Mass.: Harvard University Press, 1995), 361.

34. John Green, Paul Herrnson, Lynda Powell, and Clyde Wilcox, "Individual Congressional Campaign Contributors: Wealthy, Conservative—and Reform-Minded," working paper.

35. Ibid., 2–3.

36. Center for Responsive Politics, *The Big Picture: Who Paid for the Last Election?* http://www.crp.org/pubs/bigpicture/blio/bpbliopac.html. Data for the 1997–98 election are not available at this time.

37. Ibid.

38. Thomas Ferguson and Joel Rogers, *Right Turn: The Decline of the Democrats and the Future of American Politics* (New York: Hill and Wang, 1986); Thomas Gais, *Improper Influence: Campaign Finance Law, Political Interest Groups, and the Problem of Equality* (Ann Arbor, Michigan: University of Michigan Press, 1998).

39. Robert S. Erikson, Gerald C. Wright, and John McIver, *Statehouse Democracy: Public Opinion and Policy in the American States* (New York: Cambridge University Press, 1993).

40. The information comes from the state party accounts filed with the respective state agencies; it does not include information filed on joint federal-state accounts.

41. This is true whether you look at the overall amount raised or at the average amount raised by Republican and Democratic incumbents.

42. Center for Responsive Politics, *The Big Picture.*

43. John F. Bibby and Thomas Holbrook, "Parties and Elections," in Virginia Gray, Russel Hanson, and Herbert Jacob, editors, *Politics in the American States: A Comparative Analysis,* seventh edition (Washington, D.C.: Congressional Quarterly Press, 1999).

44. National Conference of State Legislatures, "Ballot Questions 1998," October 30, 1998, http://www.ncsl.org/statevote98/initref98.htm.

45. Voter pamphlets describing the ballot questions are apparently not very widely used by voters. See Thomas E. Cronin, *Direct Democracy* (Cambridge, Mass.: Harvard University Press, 1989).

46. Oregon Secretary of State's Office, "Secretary of State Studies Money in Initiative Signature-Gathering: Almost $2.5 Million Paid in 1996 Election Cycle," News Release, March 31, 1997, http://www.sos.state.or.us/executive/pressrel/970331.htm.

47. John S. Shockley, *The Initiative Process in Colorado Politics: An Assessment* (Boulder: Bureau of Governmental Research and Service, University of Colorado, 1980); Steven D. Lydenberg, *Bankrolling Ballots, Update 1980: The Role of Business in Financing Ballot Question Campaigns* (New York: Council on Economic Priorities, 1981); Daniel H. Lowenstein, "Campaign Spending and Ballot Propositions: Recent Experience, Public Choice Theory, and the First Amendment, *UCLA Law Review* 29 (February 1982); Betty H. Zisk, *Money, Media, and the Grass Roots: State Ballot Issues and the Electoral Process* (Newbury Park, Calif.: Sage Publications, 1987); Shaun Bowler, Todd Donovan, and Trudi Happ, "Ballot Propositions and Information Costs: Direct Democracy and the Fatigued Voter," *Western Political Quarterly* 45 (1992), 559–568; Thomas E. Cronin, *Direct Democracy* (Cambridge, Mass.: Harvard University Press, 1989); David Magelby, *Direct Legislation* (Baltimore: Johns Hopkins Press, 1984).

48. Shockley, *The Initiative Process in Colorado*; Steven D. Lydenberg, *Bankrolling Ballots, Update 1980: The Role of Business in Financing Ballot Question Campaigns* (New York: Council on Economic Priorities, 1981); Daniel H. Lowenstein, "Campaign Spending and Ballot Propositions"; Betty H. Zisk, *Money, Media and the Grass Roots*.

49. Thomas E. Cronin, *Direct Democracy*, 111.

50. Political Reform Division, *California's Statewide Ballot Measures: 1992 General Election Campaign* (Sacramento, Calif.: California Secretary of State, 1993), 24.

51. Thomas E. Patterson, *Out of Order* (New York: Alfred A. Knopf, 1993).

5

Contributors

In the previous chapter I discussed how campaign money is distributed and how it affects the fortunes of candidates. Since money is a key to candidates' electoral fortunes, the sources of campaign money are, by necessity, important. This circumstance has led many observers and much of the public to conclude that campaign contributions "buy" lawmakers. It is a conclusion that is disputed by others—including contributors and many political scientists—who argue that campaign contributions merely buy access to lawmakers. The reality, I think, lies somewhere in between. Contributors do wield some influence. But, in a pluralistic democracy, the fact that contributors wield some influence is not in itself a reason to be concerned about campaign finance. What is of concern is whether those who gain influence through contributions represent limited segments of society. When such is the case, the pluralist system becomes less representative and less democratic, favoring those organized interests that have the means to contribute significant amounts of money to the campaigns of lawmakers and slighting those that do not. The real and perceived political inequality that results adversely affects the legitimacy of the political process.

In the last chapter I demonstrated how the lack of attention to political equality in elections undermines the representational function of elections. The purpose of this chapter is to show the impact of loosely regulated private financing of campaigns on the representative character of the pluralist aspects of government in the United States. There are two prerequisites for this task: first, determining whether contributions can influence the lawmaking process; and second, determining whether those who contribute most heavily to campaigns represent limited segments of the U.S. society.

Context is critical here. The democratic system in the United States is pluralistic. As I pointed out in Chapter 1, a pluralistic democracy is one in which those with common interests organize into groups in order to influence the course of government. Governments in pluralistic democracies are structured so that power is fragmented, which is certainly the case in the U.S. system. This arrangement allows interest groups multiple points of access to the policy-making process.[1] In a pluralist system, neither interest-group influence nor influence through contributions is "bad" in its own right—such activities are part of the natural order of things in a pluralistic democracy. Influence through contributions is a problem only if that influence consistently tips the balance in favor of certain interests in society by increasing the advantage held by those organized segments of society that have an advantage in one key political resource—money.

The Relationship Between Contributors and Lawmakers

Campaign contributions do not outright "buy" politicians or their votes on legislation. Money does not rule. On the other hand, campaign contributions are not inconsequential. Instead, from what we know of the exchange between contributor and lawmaker and governmental decision making, it seems that the reality lies somewhere in between these two alternatives. In this section I will try to show why that is so, first by discussing the nature of the exchange between contributor and lawmaker, then by discussing what is involved in the decisions made by government, and finally by looking at the results of political-science research.

The Exchange

The image most people seem to have of the exchange between contributor and lawmaker is probably something akin to selling one's soul to the devil; PACs seek out desperate candidates and proffer the coveted campaign money in exchange for their political souls. This lurid picture is not a very accurate one. First, it is often the lawmakers who are chasing after the contributors and shaking them down for campaign contributions.[2] Second, all contributors do not follow the strategy implicit in this scenario when trying to influence governmental decisions. Most large contributors do follow a legislative strategy—that is, they try to influence the legislative process by giving to those candidates who are most likely to be in power after an election—i.e., the incumbents.[3] This strategy gives these groups access to the lawmakers. The access gives them an opportunity to persuade lawmakers. The money enhances the group's position since the lawmakers may feel a certain amount of indebtedness from accepting contributions.

Some groups, however, follow an electoral strategy in making their contributions to candidates. They attempt to influence government policy by changing the type of candidate elected. This strategy means supporting candidates who already agree with them. In this case, there is no need to use money to try to persuade a lawmaker to vote against his/her conscience or constituency. Labor and ideological groups tend to follow this strategy, making contributions almost exclusively to candidates in agreement with their politics, including nonincumbent candidates.

Most business and professional groups tend to follow a legislative strategy, contributing not just to those with whom they agree but also to incumbents who are less friendly to their interests but are likely to remain in power.[4]

The Lawmaking Process

The writers of the U.S. Constitution created a government in which power was separated among different branches (and even separated within those branches) and divided between national and state governments. This dispersal of power requires a great deal of bargaining and compromise among the various participants. A change in government policy at the national level requires the consent of (or at least the absence of active hostility between) the leaders of the majority parties in the House and Senate. It requires the consent of House and Senate committee and subcommittee members (especially the chairs) who have jurisdiction over the policy. In the House the process requires consent of the Rules Committee before the proposed policy change (a bill) can make it to the floor, where all House members are asked to cast a series of votes on the bill and on proposed amendments to the bill. In the Senate it must not face strong objections from any senator who could block it with a filibuster before a vote on the floor is even taken. It must be signed by the president and implemented by the bureaucracy, usually with cooperation of state and local governments and their bureaucracies. And the policy change will often be interpreted by the courts, whose job it is to determine whether the legislated change is Constitutional.

During the decision-making stage of each branch, the other branches and other governments often try to influence the process. Presidents threaten vetoes. Congressional committees review the implementation of the law by the bureaucracy. State and local officials lobby Congress and the White House. The U.S. Solicitor General and the state attorneys general represent the executive branch before the courts.

Even with this simplified version of the process, it should be obvious that our system makes it very difficult to change the law. It is much easier to block a change in law than to bring about change. Change requires agreement from so many actors within the system. Agreement forces compromise. Thus, the political system in the U.S. has a conservative bias—a bias in favor of the status quo—that favors groups that prefer inaction. That is the way it was designed.

Interests in society make use of the fragmented nature of the system to gain access to those with power. And campaign contributions are one way for interests to try to establish access. With that access interest groups try to make it clear to lawmakers how government action or inaction will affect their well-being and why it is in the interest of the lawmaker to represent their group's concerns. This presentation of the interest's concerns is backed explicitly or implicitly by the power of the interest. Interest groups can conduct polls and give the results to lawmakers. They can mobilize their membership, mounting letter-writing (or faxing or E-mail) campaigns. They can mount paid advertising campaigns to sway public opinion. And they can make or withhold campaign contributions.

The interest groups that lobby the lawmaker are not the only interests considered by the lawmaker when deciding how to vote, propose bills, propose amendments to bills, offer changes in the language of bills, issue regulations, and so on. Depending on the topic of the law change, lawmakers could feel pressure from a multitude of other interests.[5] Members of Congress may hear from other government officials such as the president, cabinet officials, or state governors. They could also feel pressure from their own party leaders or fellow members of Congress. They could feel pressure from their state via their governor, state legislative leaders, city mayors, or other members of their state's congressional delegation. They must consider their constituency and their own personal political beliefs. If they are acting on legislation that they know is or could be of great interest to those who elected them, they will act accordingly. Finally, most people who pursue a public career do so with a set of beliefs or ideals regarding what government ought to be doing, that is, a political ideology. That ideology also affects the lawmakers' decisions. Figure 5.1 summarizes the possible forces that could influence a lawmaker's activities.

The simplistic notion of moneyed interests dominating the political process just doesn't capture the complexity of the lawmaking process and the multitude of forces that attempt to influence it. Moneyed interests cannot prevail all the time in such a system. There are conditions under which they will have more or less influence in governmental decision making. If they face significant opposition from the other forces in the process—such as the president, party leaders, or the public—then their influence will diminish. If the outcome moneyed interests seek does not generate much concern among other interests or powerful actors, then they will likely exercise proportionately greater influence. If they are pushing for a significant change in government policy, they will have less influence than if their goal is to block change. To get government to enact change, they will need to have support that extends beyond the scope of those whom they contribute money to (unless they are an exceptionally wealthy group), and they must bargain and make compromises. If they want to block change, they only need to influence one step of the process to stop it.

FIGURE 5.1   **Lawmaking model: factors that affect the decisions and
activity of lawmakers**

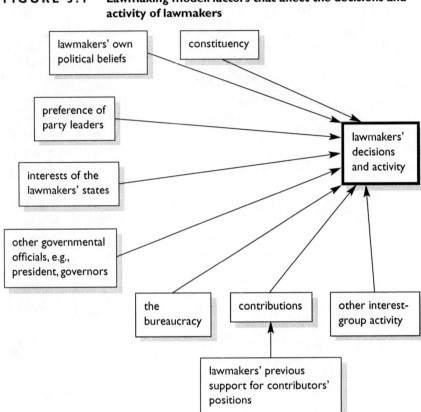

Research Findings

The nature of the influence of campaign contributions on governmental decisions depends upon the conditions under which the decisions are made. Campaign contributions can be used to influence the outcome of governmental decisions, but we have to think about when and where the contributors can have the
greatest effect. Political scientists have investigated the link between contributions
and legislators' decisions on a number of different issues in different stages of the
lawmaking process in the U.S. Congress.

Like testing for the impact of money on elections, testing for a link between contributions and votes requires the development of a model that reflects that complexity of the lawmaking process. Such a model must account for the impact of other forces on the lawmakers' decisions—political party, the lawmaker's own ideology, the preferences of the lawmaker's constituents, interests of their state, the president's position, and so on (see Figure 5.1). The model also has to take into account the goal of the interest groups—whether they seek a major or minor change in the law or whether they seek to block changes in the law. And the model also has to take into account the possibility that contributions are given to lawmakers because they have supported the contributor's positions in the past as opposed to being given for the promise of future support.

While journalistic accounts of the role of campaign contributions have long claimed that contributions lead to influence,[6] there is less certainty in findings of scientific research utilizing sophisticated models. A study by Janet Grenzke of contributions made by ten organizations (and their 120 affiliated PACs) to members of the U.S. House concluded that campaign contributions "generally do not maintain or change House members' voting patterns."[7] A study by John Wright found an indirect link between contributions and votes on the House Ways and Means Committee.[8] Campaign contributions helped to explain the number of lobbying contacts with committee members; committee votes were best explained "by the number of lobbying contacts members received from groups on each side of the issue."[9] In other words, money purchased access, and access led to influence. Richard Hall's and Frank Wayman's study of the activities of the members of three House committees on three issues (the Dairy Stabilization Act, the Job Training Partnership Act, and the Natural Gas Market Policy Act) found a more significant role for money.[10] Hall and Wayman examined the participation of members on these committees. Participation included attendance, voting, speaking, offering amendments, authorship of parts of the legislation, and behind-the-scenes negotiations. They found a significant correlation between campaign contributions and the level of activity of the committee members supporting the contributing interest on these three issues. Yet another study, one on the vote on the McClure-Volkmer Bill—a bill that loosened the laws controlling the sale of firearms in 1986—found that "the NRA's and Handgun Control's prevote campaign contributions affected member's subsequent votes, even when other variables, including ideology, member's prior position, and constituency characteristics, are held constant."[11]

All of these studies focused on the U.S. Congress. Because of the difficulty of obtaining campaign-finance and role-call votes, very little research has been done on the role of campaign contributions on policy making in state governments.

One study of overall interest group influence in the states, however, concluded that "the factor that appears to have an increasing influence in strengthening the effect of groups is campaign contributions. The larger the number and the greater the percentage of contribution that are given directly by groups to candidates, the more impact the group system appears to have."[12]

The findings of the scientific research fit well with the prior discussion of the lawmaking process. Campaign contributions are not going to buy votes on legislation in all instances. There is some indication, however, that campaign contributions are associated with votes on the floor or in committee in some cases (sometimes indirectly). There is also evidence that contributions are associated with the activity of legislators on behalf of or against a piece of legislation in committees. As is the case with elections, where money alone does not determine the outcome, money is an important but not the sole determining factor when it comes to lawmaking decisions. Because money does at times influence the lawmaking process, those who can contribute significant amounts of it to various office holders do have an advantage in the pluralist system, especially over the long run. In other words, financial contributions to campaigns do tilt political representation in the U.S. pluralist system; the question of who makes those contributions and what sectors of society they represent is, then, a significant one.

Who Gives?

As I pointed out in Chapter 3, campaign-finance law allows for a very high degree of freedom for those who have money to give to campaigns. U.S. governments have passed laws that set limits on contributions that individuals, PACs, corporations, and labor unions can give in an attempt to reduce undue influence by the largest campaign contributors. These laws, however, have not been very effective in reducing the involvement of moneyed interests in campaigns.[13] Federal, state, and some local governments set their own limits on campaign contributions. The federal government bans direct contributions from corporations and labor unions and limits individual contributions to $1,000 per election and PAC contributions to $5,000 per election. These limits have little effect, however, since large contributors can give unlimited soft money and spend unlimited amounts of money on independent campaigns for or against candidates or on issue advocacy (see Chapter 3). Fourteen states allow for individuals and PACs to give unlimited amounts of money to candidate campaigns. The rest have various limits on either individual contributions—ranging from $100 to $20,000—or on the aggregate contributions. Twenty-five states allow direct corporate contributions, and eight of those states put no limit on those contributions.[14] Clearly, then, there are many ways and places where wealthy interests can contribute a significant amount of money.

Given this reality, we should expect to find that the money in the electoral system comes disproportionately from wealthier sectors of society, including wealthy individuals, businesses, and professionals. In this section I test those expectations by analyzing the level of campaign contributions made by organizations and individuals to candidates, parties, and ballot-measure campaigns.

Most of the money contributed to campaigns in the United States comes from a narrow segment of our society: businesses, professionals, and the wealthy. This is true whether you look at contributions to national campaigns and political parties, state legislative candidates, gubernatorial candidates, or ballot measure campaigns.

Using data from the Center for Responsive Politics (CRP), I have graphed, in Figure 5.2, the total contributions to federal campaigns from various interests

· ·

FIGURE 5.2   Contributions to federal campaigns by interest and type of contribution, 1995–1996

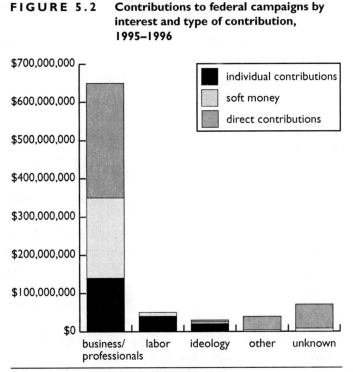

Source: Center for Responsive Politics, *Who Paid for the Last Election: The Big Picture*, http://www.crp.org/pubs/bigpicture/default.htm.

during the 1996 election cycle.[15] Contributions in the chart include direct contributions to candidates from PACs, individual contributions, and soft-money contributions. Business/professional and labor categories in the chart are self-explanatory. Ideological interests include single-interest groups (such as those concerned with abortion, handguns, and the environment), leadership PACs (committees established by party leaders), and conservative or liberal groups (such as Eagle Forum and the National Committee for an Effective Congress). The figure shows how business and professional interests dominate the realm of financing elections. Contributions from businesses and professionals were eleven times the amount contributed by labor and nineteen times the amount contributed by ideological groups.

In Figure 5.3 I graphically present the CRP's analysis of the source of direct contributions to federal candidates, broken down by more specific interests. The finance, insurance, and real-estate businesses outstrip any other sectors in direct contributions. In this comparison labor looks well represented, but that appearance is misleading because such a large proportion of business and professionals contributions are given in the form of soft money or in individual contributions (see Figure 5.2) that are not included in this chart. In order to show the advantage business has in direct contributions over one of its frequent opponents in the lawmaking process—environmental groups—I have charted the direct contributions made by environmentalists in Figure 5.3 (environmentalist contributions were included as part of the contributions by ideological groups in Figure 5.2). When compared to all business groups, the contributions by environmentalists barely register.

Businesses tend to be dominant among the soft-money contributors. Table 5.1 lists the top ten soft-money contributors in the 1997–98 election cycle. Every single one of these contributors is a corporation. Two of the top five—Philip Morris and RJR Nabisco—are in the tobacco business, an industry that has been trying to fend off government penalties and regulation.

In addition to the enormous imbalance in favor of business and professional interests, the reader should ask, Who is missing in this analysis? Which interests are not being represented in the campaign-finance system? To answer that question, you need to think about what interests run counter to those of business and professional interests (other than the seriously outfinanced labor organizations). What about consumers? Clients of the legal and health professions? Nonunionized laborers? The poor? As Bob Dole once said, "There is no welfare mother's PAC." These sorts of interests tend to be underrepresented in a pluralist democracy because they lack resources or ability to form groups. The importance of money coming from other interests that do form groups accentuates these

• •

FIGURE 5.3   **Direct contributions to federal candidates from PACs and individuals by affiliation, 1995–1996**

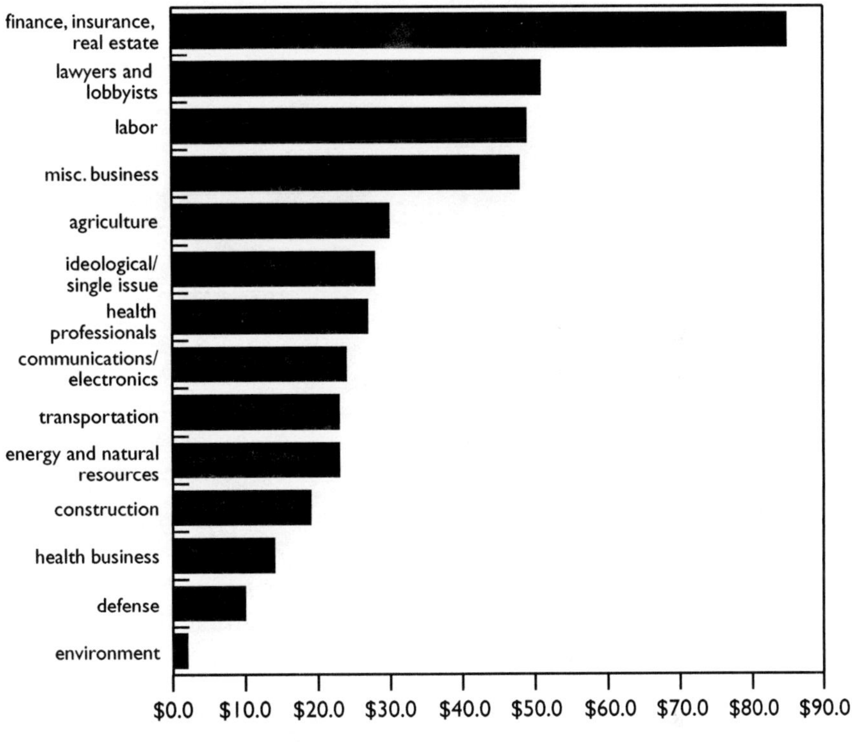

Source: Center for Responsive Politics, *Who Paid for the Last Election: The Big Picture,*
http://www.crp.org/pubs/bigpicture/default.htm.

groups' disadvantage in the system, shifting the system even further from the ideal of pluralism by making the system less representative of the public as a whole.

There are other lopsided matchups on a host of specific issues. For example, groups opposed to gun control contributed much more than the only gun-control group that made contributions, Handgun Control Inc. That difference is quite evident in Figure 5.4, in which I compare the contributions made by pro- and anti-gun-control interests. Pro-Israel interests gave $4,218,716 in an attempt to shape American foreign policy in the Middle East.[16] There were no counter-vailing contributions from Arab interests.

TABLE 5.1

Top ten soft-money contributors, 1997–1998 (through October 1, 1998)

Contributor:	Amount:
Philip Morris	$1,779,845
Amway Corp	$1,312,500
AT&T	$844,743
American Financial Group (insurance)	$735,000
RJR Nabisco	$701,422
Bell Atlantic	$683,169
Blue Cross/Blue Shield	$671,950
Freddie Mac (real estate)	$625,000
Walt Disney Co.	$596,778
Travelers Group (insurance)	$587,829

Source: Center for Responsive Politics, *Who's Paying for This Election: The Big Picture,*
http://www.crp.org/whospaying/soft/topdonors.htm.

The overrepresentation of businesses and professionals found at the national level prevails at the state level as well. In Figure 5.5 I present the sources of affiliated contributions to state house candidates for the 1991 and 1992 elections in seventeen states.[17] Businesses (either through direct contributions or through PACs) make up the bulk of contributions to state legislative candidates. Business contributions constitute over half of the contributions in fourteen of the seventeen states. They constitute about three-fourths of the contributions in New Jersey. Combined contributions from businesses and professionals constitute over 60 percent of affiliated contributions made in every state analyzed.

The domination of business and professional interests can also be found in gubernatorial races. I have obtained a breakdown of contributions to gubernatorial campaigns in Virginia in 1997 and Wisconsin in 1998. I present the distribution of the sources of those contributions in Figure 5.6. In these two contests businesses far outstrip their closest rivals as a source of campaign money.

An analysis of contributions to city races in Chicago shows the dominance of business interests at that level, too. In figure 5.7 I present a chart of the source of contributions to city-council campaigns and to mayoral campaigns in the 1995 election. Businesses make up over 75 percent of the money in these Chicago elections.

Business interests also dominate the contributions going to ballot measure campaigns—that is, campaigns to support or oppose initiatives or referenda.

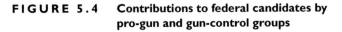

FIGURE 5.4 **Contributions to federal candidates by pro-gun and gun-control groups**

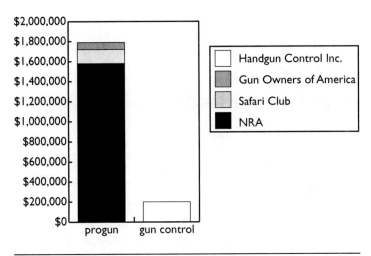

Source: Center for Responsive Politics, *Who Paid for the Last Election: The Big Picture*, http://www.crp.org/pubs/bigpicture/default.htm.

Studies of past initiative and referenda campaigns have shown that they are financed mostly from businesses.[18] I examined contributions to recent ballot measures in two states and found the same pattern. In Figure 5.8, I present the breakdown of contributions to ballot-measure campaigns in Nebraska in 1996.[19] The committees campaigning for or against the six ballot measures received 76 percent of their contributions from businesses. In Figure 5.9, I present the distribution of contributions made to proposition committees (both single and multi-proposition committees) in California in 1996. The California Secretary of State identified only those contributions of $10,000 or more (an astounding fact that says something about the source of this money in its own right). Contributions by businesses that were at least $10,000 constituted 45 percent of all the money raised by California proposition committees in 1996. Of the money raised by these committees, 81 percent came in contributions of $10,000 or greater! After businesses, law firms and individuals constituted the bulk of itemized contributions over $10,000. It can be safely assumed that individual contributions in these amounts came from wealthy businesspersons or professionals, so the estimate of

FIGURE 5.5 **Affiliated contributions to state house campaigns, 1991 (New Jersey and Mississippi) and 1992 elections (all other states)**

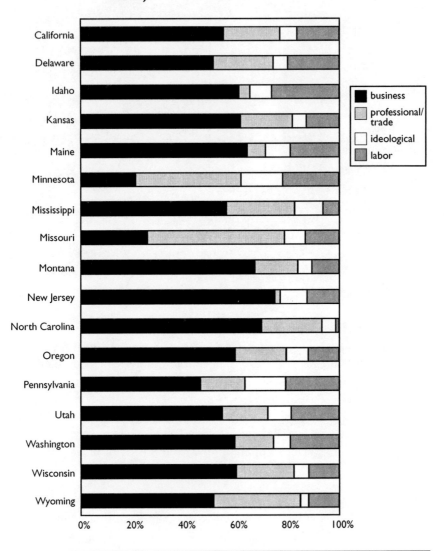

Source: Author.

FIGURE 5.6 Campaign contributions to 1997 Virginia gubernatorial campaign (Beyer v. Gilmore) and 1998 Wisconsin gubernatorial campaign

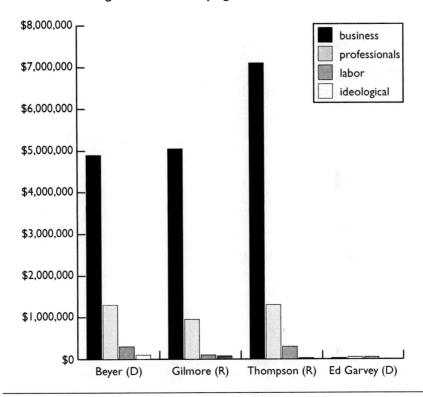

Sources: Virginia Public Access Project, http://www.crp.org/vpap/gov19997G.htm; Wisconsin Co-operative Campaign Finance Database, a joint project of the Wisconsin Democracy Campaign and Wisconsin Citizen Action, funded by the Joyce Foundation, http://www.crp.org/wdc/.

the proportion of money coming from business concerns in all likelihood underestimates the role business interest play in California ballot-measure campaigns. Moreover, individuals like Bruce Springstein and Johnnie Cochran can afford to give $10,000 or more (both made contributions in the amount of $10,000 to committees opposing Proposition 209, the anti-affirmative-action proposition),[20] but most people cannot.

Finally, a look at individual contributors reveals a disproportionate representation of those of higher socioeconomic status. A recent survey found that about 24

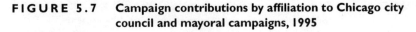

FIGURE 5.7   Campaign contributions by affiliation to Chicago city council and mayoral campaigns, 1995

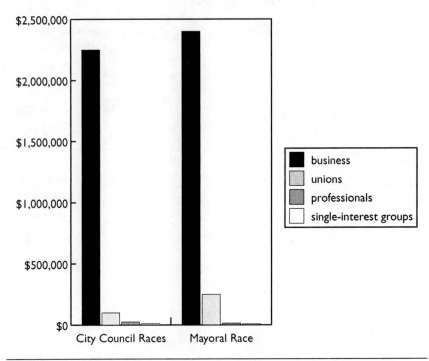

Source: Anthony Gierzynski, Paul Kleppner, and James Lewis, "The Price of Democracy: Financing Chicago's 1995 City Elections" (Chicago: Private Money in Local Elections, 1996).

percent of respondents claimed to have given campaign contributions to candidates or political parties during the 1988 election year, averaging about $58 dollars per respondent.[21] While this level of participation may seem encouraging, consider the number of contributions of this size that candidates and parties would have to raise to compete in a campaign-finance system that posts the levels of fund-raising evident in this chapter and the previous ones. These small contributions do not add up to much, and candidates and parties depend much more heavily on big contributors. Those who make such contributions come from a very exclusive economic elite. Only 5 percent of the public gave $250 or more in 1988.[22] And the strongest predictor of how much someone contributes is his or her family income.[23]

••

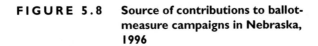

FIGURE 5.8   **Source of contributions to ballot-measure campaigns in Nebraska, 1996**

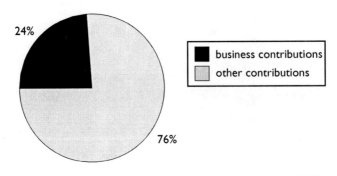

24%

■ business contributions
▨ other contributions

76%

Finances for ballot measures that successfully got onto the election ballot. Measures included constitutional amendments to

• instruct Nebraska's congressional delegation to support term limits
• lower the number of signatures required to qualify a ballot measure
• make education the "paramount duty" of the state
• establish property-tax limits
• authorize off-track parimutuel betting on horseraces
• authorize members of legislature to participate in state employee benefit plans

Source: Nebraska Accountability and Disclosure Commission, *The 1996 State of Nebraska Primary and General Elections: A Summary of Political Campaign Finance,* 1998.

A study of contributors to 1996 congressional campaigns found that 95 percent of those making contributions of $200 or more had family incomes of $50,000 or more (see Figure 5.10).[24] The median income in the U.S. in 1996 was $35,172 (the median is the amount at which half of the population made less and half made more).[25] Some 46 percent of contributors came from households with family incomes of $250,000 or more.

A study of contributors to presidential candidates during the nomination phase identified a pool of contributors who give large contributions to candidates year after year. These contributors "are generally white, male, well-educated, affluent, and active in contributing at several levels of government."[26] Some 60 percent of the contributors in this pool had family incomes greater than $100,000, and 30 percent of those had family incomes greater than $250,000. Furthermore, among that pool are individuals who are part of candidates' fund-raising networks and

••

FIGURE 5.9   Contributions to ballot-measure campaigns in California, 1996

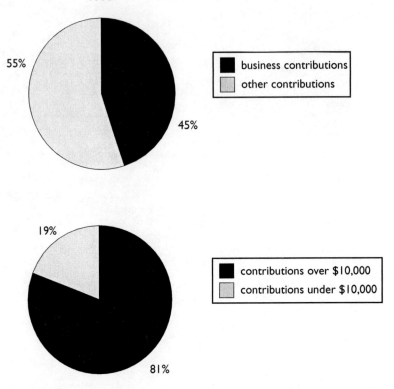

Figures include contributions to both single-proposition committees and multiple-proposition committees.

- 192 (Seismic Retrofit Bond Act)
- 209 (affirmative-action ban)
- 212 (campaign-finance reform)
- 213 (limitation on recovery to felons, uninsured motorists, drunk drivers)
- 214 (health care, consumer protection)
- 215 (medical use of marijuana)

Source: California Secretary of State, "Financing California's Statewide Ballot Measures: 1996 Primary and General Elections," http://www.ss.ca.gov/prd/bmc96/coverbm96.htm.

who solicit money on behalf of candidates, a service that undoubtedly gives them some pull with the candidates. These "solicitors" are even more affluent than the pool of contributors, and many of them are "lawyer-lobbyists who hope to repre-

FIGURE 5.10 Family income of congressional donors

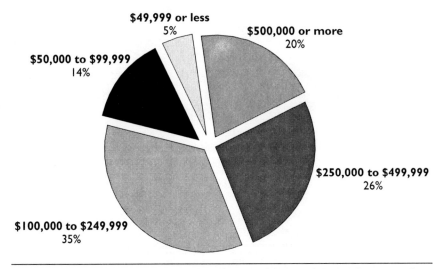

Source: John Green, Paul Herrnson, Lynda Powell, and Clyde Wilcox, "Individual Congressional Campaign Contributors: Wealthy, Conservative—and Reform-Minded," working paper.

sent their clients to the candidate for whom they are soliciting."[27] Individual contributions are clearly not an avenue for the average citizen to participate in the U.S. campaign-finance system.

Conclusion

In 1960 the political theorists E. E. Schattschneider wrote, "The flaw in the pluralist heaven is that the heavenly chorus sings with a strong upper-class accent."[28] The material presented and discussed in this chapter clearly shows that campaign-finance practices in the United States exacerbate that bias. Campaign contributions give greater access and in many cases greater influence to the person or group that makes the contribution. Most of the money contributed to candidates, parties, and ballot committees comes from a narrow set of interests: business interests, professionals, and wealthy individuals. These facts suggest that the pluralist system favors a narrow set of interests and underrepresents the full diversity of the American polity. This bias extends beyond campaign contributions to the entire lobbying enterprise. Darrell West's and Burdett Loomis's study of interest-group activity (including mass-media campaigns) concluded, "Schattschneider's heavenly chorus sings with more of an upper-class accent than ever before. Large, well-funded interests are crowding out consumer groups, public-interest groups, political parties, and even broad-based social movements."[29] The political freedom allowed contributors clearly leads to unequal political representation, making the system less democratic and weakening the legitimacy of the government.

Notes

1. Robert A. Dahl, *Who Governs?* (New Haven: Yale University Press, 1961); and, Dahl, *Democracy and Its Critics* (New Haven: Yale University Press, 1989).

2. Frank J. Sorauf, *Inside Campaign Finance: Myths and Realities* (New Haven: Yale University Press, 1992).

3. For a study of PAC strategies, see Robert Biersack, Paul S. Herrnson, and Clyde Wilcox, editors, *Risky Business? PAC Decisionmaking in Congressional Elections* (New York: M. E. Sharpe, 1994).

4. Biersack et al., *Risky Business?*

5. See Aage R. Clausen, *How Congressmen Decide: A policy focus* (New York: St. Martin's Press, 1973); Malcolm E. Jewell, *Representation in State Legislatures* (Lexington: University Press of Kentucky, 1982); and John W. Kingdon, *Congressmen's Voting Decisions,* second edition (New York: Harper and Row, 1981).

6. See, for example, Elizabeth Drew, *Politics and Money: The New Road to Corruption* (New York: Macmillan, 1983); Phillip M. Stern, *The Best Congress Money Can Buy* (New York: Pantheon, 1988).

7. Janet M. Grenzke, "PACs and the Congressional Supermarket: the Currency Is Complex," *American Journal of Political Science* 33 (1988), 19.

8. John R. Wright, "Contributions, Lobbying, and Committee Voting in the U.S. House of Representatives," *American Political Science Review* 84 (1990): 417–438.

9. John R. Wright, "Contributions, Lobbying, and Committee Voting in the U.S. House of Representatives," 433.

10. Hall, Richard L., and Frank W. Wayman, "Buying Time: Moneyed Interests and the Mobilization Bias in Congressional Elections," *American Political Science Review* 84 (1990): 797–820.

11. Laura I. Langbein and Mark A. Lotwis, "The Political Efficacy of Lobbying and Money: Gun Control in the U.S. House, 1986," *Legislative Studies Quarterly* 15 (August 1990), 413–440.

12. Clive S. Thomas and Ronald J. Hrebenar, "Interest Group Influence in the States," in Virginia Gray and Herbert Jacob, editors, *Politics in the American States: A Comparative Analysis* (Washington, D.C.: Congressional Quarterly Press, 1996).

13. For a good study of the effectiveness (or ineffectiveness) of campaign-finance limits, see Michael J. Malbin and Thomas L. Gais, *The Day After Reform: Sobering Campaign Fi-*

nance Lessons from the American States (Albany, N.Y.: The Rockefeller Institute Press, 1998).

14. The Council of State Governments, *The Book of the States, 1996–97 Edition*, Vol. 31 (Lexington: The Council of State Governments, 1996), 177–194.

15. The Center for Responsive Politics analyzed all campaign contributions—from PACs, individuals, corporations, labor unions, and parties—during the 1996 electoral cycle and affiliated each contribution with a set of interests or sector of the economy. Their assignment of contributions helps us get a better picture of where the money in federal elections comes from than the data reported by the FEC. The FEC presents their data according to legal multicandidate committees (PACs), which do not necessarily identify the interests (nonconnected committees in particular can represent a number of different interests including business; BIPAC [the Business Industry PAC], for example, is categorized as a nonconnected PAC). Additionally, individual contributions recorded by the FEC are not categorized by the interest of the giver. For a description of their methodology, see http://www.crp.org/pubs/bigpicture/overview/methodol.htm.

16. The Center for Responsive Politics, "Ideological/Single Issue," http://www.crp.org/pubs/bigpicture/profiles/bp.profile12.html.

17. This analysis excludes individual and party contributions and intercandidate transfers.

18. John S. Shockley, *The Initiative Process in Colorado Politics: An Assessment* (Boulder: Bureau of Governmental Research and Service, University of Colorado, 1980); Steven D. Lydenberg, *Bankrolling Ballots, Update 1980: The Role of Business in Financing Ballot Question Campaigns* (New York: Council on Economic Priorities, 1981); Daniel H. Lowenstein, "Campaign Spending and Ballot Propositions: Recent Experience, Public Choice Theory, and the First Amendment, *UCLA Law Review* 29 (1982); Betty H. Zisk, *Money, Media, and the Grass Roots: State Ballot Issues and the Electoral Process* (Newbury Park, Calif.: Sage Publications, 1987).

19. The analysis is of ballot measures that qualified for the ballot. Measures that failed to obtain enough signatures were not included, though the proportion of the contributions to these failed measures from businesses is not substantially different from the successful ballot measures.

20. California Secretary of State, "Financing California's Statewide Ballot Measures: 1996 Primary and General Elections," http://www.ss.ca.gov/prd/bmc96/coverbm96.htm.

21. Sidney Verba, Kay Lehman Schlozman, and Henry E. Brady, *Voice and Equality: Civic Voluntarism in American Politics* (Cambridge, Mass.: Harvard University Press, 1995), 51.

22. Verba et al., *Voice and Equality*, 54.

23. Ibid., 361.

24. John Green, Paul Herrnson, Lynda Powell, and Clyde Wilcox, "Individual Congressional Campaign Contributors: Wealthy, Conservative—and Reform-Minded," working paper.

25. U.S. Census Bureau, "Changes in Median Household Income: 1969 to 1996," http://www.census.gov/hhes/www/mednhhldincome.html.

26. Clifford W. Brown Jr., Lynda W. Powell, and Clyde Wilcox, *Serious Money: Fundraising and Contributing in Presidential Nomination Contest* (New York: Cambridge University Press, 1995), 49.

27. Ibid., 142.

28. E. E. Schattschneider, *The Semi-Sovereign People: A Realist's View of Democracy in America* (New York: Holt, Rinehart and Winston, 1960), 35.

29. Darrell M. West and Burdett A. Loomis, *The Sound of Money: How Political Interests Get What They Want* (New York: W. W. Norton, 1999), 228.

6

Conclusion

Why should this matter, we are asked by those all too eager to equate freedom of speech with freedom to spend. It should matter because political equality is the essence of democracy, and an electoral system driven by big money is one lacking in political equality.

—Senator Susan Collins (R.–Maine)[1]

To claim that campaign spending is a legitimate exercise of free speech is to deny the constitutional principle that each one of us counts.

—Senator Dale Bumpers (D.–Arkansas)[2]

I WROTE THIS BOOK to encourage an understanding of campaign finance based on the context in which campaign-finance activities take place and an understanding of the underlying conflict that is inherent in this issue. Campaign-finance activities affect not only elections but also the interest-group competition that is at the heart of the pluralist system in the United States. In this context, the fact that U.S. governments tend to resolve the conflict between political quality and political freedom—intrinsic in a system that privately finances its elections—in favor of the latter allows economic inequalities to become political inequalities. This is *the* problem of campaign finance in the United States. And it is a downward-spiraling problem. As political influence becomes more and more a function of wealth, political inequalities grow. Inequalities in elections—the institution that encourages all citizens to participate in government and makes that participation of equal worth—interfere with elections' ability to function effectively within the system and diminish the role they play. With elections playing a less important role in the way the polity makes its decisions, interest-group competition—the essence of pluralism—becomes more important. In that competition, campaign-finance practices further skew the system in favor of the financially advantaged interests, who gain additional influence from their role in financing lawmakers' elections. The inequality evident in elections and in government decision making, in turn, feeds public cynicism about the political system, leading citizens to drop out of the system, which further sharpens the inequalities.

The defense of the freedom to spend as part of the First Amendment right to freedom of speech has left campaign finance behavior to follow its natural tendency (discussed in Chapter 2) to flow to the points of power. This tendency, in turn, has led to an unequal distribution of political money in elections and has ceded greater political influence to moneyed interests in the U.S. system.

As I pointed out in Chapter 4, campaign-finance practices in U.S. elections favor incumbents, personally wealthy candidates, the Republican party, and the sides of ballot measures supported by business. Since money is needed in most elections to communicate with voters, these imbalances lead to lopsided campaign discourse and thus deprive voters of the chance to make meaningful and informed choices in many electoral contests. As demonstrated by recent elections, these imbalances can worsen when the power of incumbency and the legislative majority rests in the hands of the party that is ideologically aligned with the major contributors.

The important role money plays in elections confers importance on those from whom the money comes (the topic of Chapter 5). On the federal, state, and local levels it is clear that U.S. campaign money comes disproportionately from business and professional interests and, more generally, the upper-income strata of the society. While the contributions made by these interests do not allow them to always "buy" their way with government, their money does provide them with much greater advantage in the pluralist system.

The political inequality fostered by campaign-finance practices in the U.S. does not go unnoticed by the public. The people's overall confidence in government's ability to represent and respond to their concerns has declined since the 1950s and has remained low throughout the 1990s. Voter turnout, too, has declined. In 1996 less than half of the eligible electorate showed up at the polls during that presidential election year. In the 1998 midterm elections only 37 percent voted. The inequalities evident in the campaign-finance system surely feed the cynicism about the U.S. system and contribute to voter indifference. People come to feel that their vote doesn't really count so that voting is a waste of time. A recent survey provides some support for these suspicions. The survey asked respondents directly how news about questionable political fund-raising affects their sense of political efficacy and their view of the value of voting. I present the results in Figure 6.1. Almost three-fourths of the respondents said that questionable fund-raising practices make them feel that "elected officials don't care about what people like you think." And, nearly four in ten respondents said that questionable fund-raising practices make them feel that "it's not worth bothering to vote."

In Senator Collins's words, quoted at the beginning of this chapter, "Political equality is the essence of democracy." Without political equality the system drifts away from democracy—rule by the many—and toward oligarchy—rule by the few. Senator Collins's concern, which I have sought to document in this book, is that current campaign-finance practices breed political inequality from economic inequality, sapping the vitality, support, and legitimacy from U.S. democracy. The system is weighted too heavily in favor of freedom. To restore legitimacy to the system, governments at all levels need to do something to even out the balance, to restore some of the political equality that has been lost because of the system's long-standing bias in favor of the freedom to spend. In other words, there is a need to change how the U.S. system finances its political campaigns.

• •

FIGURE 6.1   **Impact of questionable
fund-raising on political
efficacy and voter
intention**

elected officials don't care what people like you think

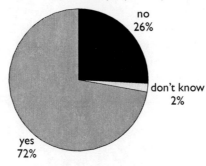

it's not worth bothering to vote

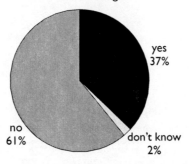

Source: Created by the author from the results of the
Money and Politics Survey, Princeton Survey Research.

Campaign-Finance Reform

As I mentioned in Chapter 3, the government in Washington has not successfully
instituted any changes to the money rules for federal elections since 1979. State
and local governments still struggle with the issue and have experimented with
many different approaches (many of which have been invalidated by the courts'
zealous protection of the freedom to spend). To conclude this book, I would like
to apply the perspective on campaign finance that I have developed in this book

to the various campaign-finance reforms that have been proposed and/or enacted in the United States.

The material in this book suggests a number of things about campaign-finance reform. It suggests an overall goal for campaign-finance reform: tipping the balance between freedom and equality toward equality in order to restore some amount of political equality that is missing in the system. It also suggests that changes should be made with an awareness of the context of campaign finance and an awareness of the principles that seem to govern campaign-finance behavior. The context is the U.S. political process, a pluralist democracy with two majoritarian institutions: elections and political parties. Campaign-finance activity takes place around elections, but it affects the competition between interest groups, the operating mechanism for pluralism. The essential principle that seems to govern campaign-finance behavior is that political money is under pressure to flow to the points of power in the system. This pressure means that money will very likely find its way around any set of regulatory barriers that are not airtight. And the judiciary's insistence on equating spending political money with freedom of speech means that no set of regulations can be airtight.

So, how does the United States achieve greater political equality under these conditions? First, some comments about the types of reforms that are not likely to succeed in light of the perspective on campaign finance outlined in this book.

Inadvisable or Impractical Reforms

Eliminating Private Money.   The goal of completely eliminating private funds from elections is based on the false premise, discussed in Chapter 1, that money "buys" public officials. That is not the problem with the campaign-finance system. Attempting to do such a thing ignores what we know of campaign-finance behavior—namely, that money gravitates to power. Experience has shown us that if you cut off or limit one channel for money, it will find another way into the system.

Unless the U.S. Supreme Court overturns *Buckley* (or it is overturned by amending the U.S. Constitution), any attempt to keep private money completely out of the campaign-finance system will fail. Full public funding—the only route left open to governments in order to achieve this goal—can create the incentives for candidates to refuse private money. Those public funds, however, must be adequate to run an effective campaign. If they are not, candidates will have the incentive to opt out of the system or to find ways to circumvent the system. The use of issue ad campaigns run by the DNC and RNC for Clinton and Dole during the 1996 presidential election is a perfect illustration of such circumvention.

Given the amount of money George W. Bush has raised as of June 1999—$36 million—speculation is rife that he will forgo the public funds and accompanying limits in his run for the Republican presidential nomination in 2000.[3] He may forgo the public funding for the general election as well, which could force the Democratic nominee to consider doing the same.

Moreover, full public funding does not allow governments to prevent groups from campaigning independently of candidates. If private funds are kept out of the candidates' coffers, the interests with money will use that money to campaign for or against candidates in a way that is protected by the courts. Under this scenario candidates face the prospect of losing control over their message to interest groups during the election. This development is already evident, especially in special elections—for example, the special election held in early 1998 to fill the vacancy created by the death of Representative Walter Capps (D.–Calif.). The election featured so much independent and issue-advocacy spending by outside interest groups—including U.S. Term Limits and Gary Bauer's The Campaign for Working Families—that the candidates felt they had lost control of the debate in the election. This is clearly a move in the wrong direction. Interest groups, not the public or the candidates who face the voters, will define the election agenda and dominate the channels of communication.

Strict Spending Limits.   Spending limits take aim, in part, at the perceived high levels of campaign spending. As I pointed out in Chapter 1, spending by itself is not the problem with campaign finance in the United States—the issue is the inequality between candidates. Unless you drop the limits down to what nonincumbent candidates can raise, you are not addressing the problem. If you do drop the levels down that far, you truly do interfere with the ability of candidates to contact and communicate with voters. For spending limits to work, they have to be set at a reasonable level and be accompanied by public funds to help nonincumbents (more on this later). And, of course, mandatory expenditure limits would not stand for long, given the court precedents.

Full Disclosure and No Limits.   At the other extreme of excluding private money is the proposal that drops all limits on contributions and instead simply requires full disclosure of the revenues and expenditures of candidates and other political committees. The logic behind this idea is that campaign-finance limits have failed and that the press and voters can police the open records and turn against candidates beholden to big money.

This proposal assumes that the sources of a candidate's money will affect voters' support for that candidate, a highly questionable assumption in view of political science's extensive knowledge of voting behavior. Voters cast their votes largely based on the personality characteristics of the candidates, party affiliation, and a few major issues. But voters typically have relatively little information about the candidates' positions on most issues. The idea that voters would punish candidates who accept large contributions does not seem likely; there has been no evidence of such voter behavior. Besides, candidates with money do have an ability to put their own spin on this information. Take Ross Perot, for example. In 1992 he cast a positive light on his lavish spending of his personal fortune on his campaign. Instead of being seen as a millionaire buying his way into office, he was seen as independent of big-money contributors.

Those practical matters aside, it should be obvious that the elimination of all restrictions would fail to address the problem of campaign finance in the United States identified in this book. This idea would do absolutely nothing to restore some of the political equality lost in the current system. Instead, more money would flow to the points of power within the system, exacerbating the bias and inequality in the system.

Some Suggestions

So where does that leave us? What can be done to tip the scales in favor of political equality in our system? A key to knowing what should be done can be found in how we view campaign-finance activity and the context in which we view it. It is crucial to understand why money is important and the principle that campaign-finance activity follows. Money is important because it is necessary for communicating with voters. To address the problems caused by the inequalities in the system, changes are needed to provide alternative means of gaining access to the public.

The principle money follows—that it will flow to the places of power in the system—means the regulation of money must be viewed differently from how it has typically been viewed. Reformers have viewed regulation as a means of *restricting* campaign-finance practices. Given what we have learned about campaign-finance behavior—that restrictions are bound to fail—I believe that a better approach is to try to *manage* the money involved in the financing of campaigns. Managing the money would mean establishing a creative set of regulations that would encourage the flow of that money to the types of organizations and for the types of purposes that enhance political equality.

Finally, the context of campaign-finance behavior must be kept in mind while considering any reform. We must remember that the system established by the founding fathers is a pluralistic democracy. Political parties and elections evolved in the system to give the public greater voice, and these two institutions, when healthy, help to counterbalance the natural biases in the pluralist system. Keeping context in mind also means keeping in mind the fact that campaign-finance activity occurs in a system shaped by many other actors and institutions. Changes to the campaign-finance system alone will not work in isolation, nor will they solve all of the problems of cynicism; low levels of political efficacy, political knowledge, and voter turnout; and the faltering legitimacy of the U.S. system.

With all of these considerations in mind, I would like to make a number of suggestions, most of which have been made elsewhere. What I suggest is all linked together because many of these changes, in isolation, will have little effect in tipping the balance away from the extreme of political freedom and toward political equality.

Alternatives for Communicating with Voters.   Since the key problem with the current system of financing elections is the inequality in resources needed to purchase contact with voters, one way to address the problem is to provide alternative ways for disadvantaged candidates to reach voters. Governments can do this by giving free television or radio time or by providing a floor of public funding for candidates.

Free radio and/or television time for candidates is something that has been part of some reforms that have been introduced in the U.S. Congress. The broadcasting industry relies upon the federal government to protect it from chaos on the airwaves. Recently television networks received a multimillion-dollar giveaway in the form of frequencies for high-definition television. Given the benefits the industry accrues from government, television and radio owners ought to return the favor in the form of free time for candidates. Since such voluntary gratitude is unlikely, the federal government could mandate such measures. Or, at the very least, the government could purchase the time for candidates.

For such free media time to be useful in communicating information, the government should attach several strings to that benefit. Candidates should have to appear and deliver their own message. This cuts down on harsh negative attacks, which are more difficult to make in person. Research has associated negative advertisements with reductions in voting.[4] Moreover, the time granted should be in blocks of time no smaller than five minutes. This allowance might force the candidates to say some substantive and useful to voters.

In lieu or in addition to free media time, governments could establish a floor of public funding for candidates. Partial public funding would allow disadvantaged candidates to purchase some contact with the voters. We know that an initial burst of spending can often serve as a springboard to electoral viability. Once they are viable, candidates can raise funds from other sources and receive assistance from their political party.

The main counterargument to such programs is that they amount to welfare for politicians. While polls show that a majority the public supports public funding in principle (see Chapter 3), the public distaste for paying taxes is magnified when it comes to paying for campaigns. This is obvious in the low levels of participation in tax checkoff and tax add-on funds established for public funding of presidential and some state elections.[5] To supplement tax checkoffs while avoiding using "taxpayer dollars," governments could find some more creative avenues for public campaign funds—for example, lobbying fees, election-filing or campaign-finance-filing fees that are a percentage of candidates' campaign revenues, and a tax on campaign-finance accounts (just think how much the public would love a tax on politicians).

Both free media time and public subsidies would go a long way to restoring the health of elections by creating greater political equality in competition. Stronger elections enhance the political voice of the citizen. Moreover, both free media time and public subsidies would reduce the debt that winning candidates would owe to contributors, thus weakening the influence of moneyed interests on policy making and restoring some faith in the legitimacy of the U.S. political system.

Reasonable Limits on Expenditures.   Free media time and public funds can be used to induce candidates to accept limits on spending. Such limits should be reasonable, based upon a formula that would allow for sufficient voter contact above and beyond the free media time. Such limits would vary with the size of the constituency and would require periodic adjustments for inflation. In order to balance out the advantages that the perquisites of office give to incumbents, limits could be set higher for challengers (as is the case in Minnesota). Political scientists have enough data on candidate spending from previous elections to be able to generate mathematical models that would show how much money a candidate would need to compete seriously for a particular office.

Some mechanisms would have to be built into the law in order to deal with extremely well financed candidates who would simply ignore the limits. If the free media time and public funds are insufficient to combat such advantages, the government could counter the wealthy candidates' spending by granting additional free media time or by providing additional public funding for the candidate's opponent(s). Of course, the simplest solution would be a Supreme Court reversal of its *Buckley* principle that spending equals speech.

Critics have argued that such spending limits would impede competition, reduce the flow of information to voters, and thus lower turnout. They also contend that limits would make it more difficult for the party out of power to win back office. In an innovative study of congressional elections, Robert Goidel, Don Gross, and Todd Shields have demonstrated that these criticisms are not supported by recent experience. These scholars found that higher spending in campaigns actually results in a more confused, less enlightened electorate. They also found that spending limits do not markedly lower voter turnout. Moreover they found that spending limits with some form of public financing would have enhanced the electoral prospects of the minority party in the 1994 and 1996 U.S. House races.[6]

Contribution Limits.   With private money still coming into a system partially financed by the public, contribution limits are needed. Such limits should reflect the overall amount of money candidates are allowed to raise under reasonable spending limits. While it is good to encourage small contributors, making candidates spend enormous amounts of time to raise a multitude of small contributions can be a problem, too. Under such systems—like the thousand-dollar limit on individual contributions to presidential-nomination campaigns—the fat cats of old are merely replaced by people who have a lot of friends with money and are willing to solicit those friends.[7]

To increase participation in the campaign-finance system, governments could encourage small contributions by providing a tax reduction for contributions up to a certain amount. Such a system is in use in Minnesota.

Limit Carryover Funds.   As I discussed in Chapter 4, one of the reasons for incumbents' advantage in fund-raising is that they are able to carry over substantial amounts of money from one campaign to the next. Limiting how much could be carried over could limit some of that advantage. Any amount over the limit would go to the fund for public financing of elections. Moreover, if incumbents know they cannot carry over funds, they would likely disburse that money to other candidates, in effect redistributing some of the money in the system from wealthy candidates to those in need.

Political Parties.   Political parties can play an important role in fostering greater political equality in the U.S. electoral system. Political parties are majoritarian institutions. Because they must put together majority coalitions during elections in order to win control of the government, they have an incentive to make broad-based appeals to the electorate and therefore to represent many of the interests that are either unrepresented or underrepresented in the current interest-group system. Hungry for votes, the parties seek to enhance public participation by getting more voters to the polls. In addition, political parties make voter participation more meaningful by organizing around a set of programs or an ideological approach to government that provides voting cues (decision shortcuts) to the public. Voters can then vote more rationally and programmatically by voting for the party, not the person. Moreover, political parties allow voters to pinpoint responsibility—usually on the party in power—for the state of the nation/state/city in an election, forcing elected officials to be more responsive to the public.

As part of an attempt to manage the flow of money through regulations, campaign-finance reforms should continue to steer money to the political parties and encourage them to use that money for activities that reinvigorate U.S. elections. As I wrote that last sentence, I could hear all of the opponents of soft money screaming out, "*What?*" Soft money, after all, has become the latest hot-button issue of campaign finance, replacing that old evil, PACs. The story about soft money, however, has focused almost exclusively on the contribution side of soft money—that is, the surge in soft money overall and the enormous checks written by corporations, lawyer-lobbyists, unions, and wealthy individuals whose largesse falls outside current federal regulations limiting contributions. That attention is well merited—for such soft money is indeed a problem—but part of the story has been ignored: the spending side of soft money, what is done with the money raised by the political parties.

Party soft money can be spent on issue advertisements—the "air war"—or on identifying, registering, and getting voters to the polling places—the "ground war." Both of these uses—especially the latter—should be seen as positive developments. Issue advertisements can strengthen the parties by allowing the parties a role in setting the electoral agenda. Identifying, registering, and getting voters to the polls increases participation—including groups underrepresented in the pluralist system—and cannot be seen as anything but positive. A recent study by David Magleby and Marianne Holt found that the money used for mobilizing voters was much more effective than that used in the "air war" during 1998 congressional races. The Democrats' success, according to Magleby and Holt, was due in part to their emphasis on the identifying, registering, and getting out the voters.

The Democratic committees' efforts resulted in an increase in turnout among Democratic voters, with an especially sharp increase among African American voters. African Americans represented 25 percent of the total turnout in 1998, up from 17 percent in the 1994 election (the previous nonpresidential election year). Magleby and Holt conclude that the success of the ground war in 1998 should lead the parties to focus on the ground war in the future.[8] That would be a positive development for elections.

Thus, soft money, properly directed, can be beneficial to the political system. Party soft-money spending enhances political equality by strengthening the political parties and increasing voter participation. I therefore oppose total prohibitions on soft money and instead recommend making soft money "hard." In other words, the federal government should regulate it, limiting the size of contributions that are allowed in order to limit the influence of the contributors.

Aside from soft money, political parties allocate their resources (their "hard money") in ways that promote greater equality in elections and thus enhance electoral competition and voter choice. Whereas interest groups tend to contribute to safe incumbents, studies of party spending show that it is channeled to competitive races, and that they are more than willing to supply the usually cash-starved challengers with campaign resources.[9] Greater party financial activity, therefore, would make electoral contests closer and reduce the hold that incumbents have on office.

Many political-party committees also recruit candidates to run for office, leaving fewer uncontested races. Thus, political-party activity already provides some evening out of the resources in elections, enhancing competition and ultimately voter choice. So, in addition to retaining but regulating soft money, new campaign-finance laws should set contribution limits to and from political parties at higher levels than other contribution limits. Such a measure would channel more of the money in the system through the parties, who by nature enhance political equality in the political system.

The attentive reader probably will have recognized a big problem with these recommendations: the significant fund-raising advantage Republican-party organizations have over Democratic organizations, as shown in Chapter 4. One possible solution is to follow the lead of some states—including Kentucky, Minnesota, North Carolina, and Utah—and provide public funding for the political parties. The national and state governments could provide grants for political parties to carry out some of their grassroots functions, namely, voter mobilization. Free television time for the parties could also level the playing field a bit.

Regulations on Issue Advocacy.   Issue-advocacy campaigns pose a major problem in any attempt to regulate campaign finance. If the above recommendations were to be adopted and issue advocacy were left unregulated, interest groups could still spend unlimited sums to skew the outcome of elections through this court-protected avenue. They would be able to set the agenda in campaigns and possibly drown out the voice of the candidates and political parties.[10] The problem with trying to come up with some way of dealing with issue advocacy is the court protection of this channel of spending.

Two things could be done, though, to rein in this type of spending. First, disclosure: issue-advocacy campaigns do not need to disclose their finances. This policy should be changed. Like soft money, issue-advocacy contributions should be brought in under federal and state campaign-finance reporting laws. Disclosure alone, however, will not solve the problems caused by these advocacy campaigns. Therefore, the definition of issue advocacy—or "express advocacy"—needs to be changed. Express-advocacy advertisements explicitly advocate the election or defeat of a clearly identified candidate through the words *vote for, oppose, support,* and so on.[11] All else is considered issue advocacy. Under court rulings the government can regulate the former but not the latter. One good suggestion is to define any advertisement as express advocacy if it contains references to any candidate for office and airs within ninety days of the election.[12] This change would significantly reduce the use of this means for skirting the campaign-finance laws and make sure the new reforms suggested here are not undercut.

Enforcement.   Changes in the laws will do no good if the agencies assigned the tasks of implementing and monitoring the law are not adequately funded and insulated from political pressure. The Federal Election Commission and state election commissions—which have been typically starved for funds—need adequate funding to sustain a staff large enough to investigate campaign-finance practices and to ensure compliance with the laws. The staff should include researchers capable of reviewing and analyzing campaign-finance practices and attorneys who can bring legal action against violators.

Providing political insulation is more problematic, especially given the recent abuse of the independent-counsel statute. It is, moreover, highly unlikely that any commission or commissioner would be entirely insulated from political pressures. Still, there are methods—evident in other independent agencies—that could enhance the enforcement capabilities of an electoral regulatory commission. Ornstein et al. propose single eight-year terms, staggered appointments, and a more powerful chair for the Federal Election Commission. They also propose allowing private legal action against violators of the law.[13] Similar structures could be set up at the state level.

A Note About Feasibility.   Many very good suggestions about campaign-finance reform are often shot down by the argument that they will never be enacted because those who have won under the current rules of the game are loath to change those rules. In addition, court disapproval always looms like a threatening cloud in the distance, ready to strike down any innovation or attempt to restore some balance between political freedom and political equality. I have made my suggestions here with a hopeful eye to the courts but have optimistically ignored the winners-don't-like-to-change-the-rules principle because I believe that eventually pressure to reform the system will be strong enough to motivate elected officials to make some changes. I saw the movement for term limits as a threat of a blunt club that may have encouraged many state lawmakers to look at the issue of campaign-finance reform as a way to reassure the restless public that there is some responsiveness to the people's will. While term-limit proposals will not threaten the U.S. Congress, massive disillusionment may take some other form and propel some change. It happened in the 1970s. It could happen again, and this time we will be wiser for the experience under the current systems.

Beyond Campaign-Finance Reform.   Just changing the money rules will not magically convert the American political process into a healthy, democratic one. There are many other aspects of the political process that could use some improvements. A full discussion of these problems and proposed solutions is beyond the scope of this book, but it is useful to go over a few to highlight the larger context of campaign-finance activity.

Some electoral procedures need to be changed to improve the health of elections. The nomination process for presidential candidates is particularly problematic and exacerbates the problems of campaign finance. I agree with Thomas Patterson that the process should be organized better; it should be shortened, and state primaries and caucuses should not be front-loaded (that is, with all the contests bunched early in the calendar).[14] Debates between major candidates could be mandated (or tied to public funds). Barriers to voting could be lifted by establishing election holidays or by making voting by mail easier (as Oregon has done). Ballot propositions should be done away with or discouraged and certainly not adopted in any other states or at the national level. Since the courts have prevented the states from regulating ballot proposition campaigns, they have become just another avenue for moneyed interests to gain an upper hand in the political process. In essence, they provide a way for moneyed interests to work around any system of campaign-finance laws that may be put in place. They have failed to live up to their promise of "direct democracy" and instead distort the process. Therefore, they should be dropped and elections returned to the issue of selecting representatives.

Laws regulating lobbying need to be rigorous enough to prevent moneyed interests from casting their shadow over legislative proceedings. And, finally, better mass-media coverage of elections could provide more alternative channels of information for voters. Journalists and news organizations must be encouraged to provide greater issue coverage. Increasing funding to public broadcasting—which already provides many excellent forums for candidates during elections—would help as well.

Democratic systems require political freedom *and* political equality in order to be seen as legitimate in the eyes of the people. The balance between these contending values has been upset, with the scales swinging nearly full-tilt toward freedom at the cost of political equality and the legitimacy of U.S. democracy. Some balance needs to be restored.

Notes

1. "Senators' Remarks on Campaign Finance Proposals," *The New York Times*, September 30, 1997, A22.

2. Dale Bumpers, "How the Sunshine Harmed Congress," *The New York Times*, January 3, 1999, WK 9.

3. Dan Balz, "One for the Record Books," *The Washington Post National Weekly Edition*, July 5 1999, 13–14.

4. Stephen Ansolabehere and Shanto Iyengar, *Going Negative: How Political Advertisements Shrink and Polarize the Electorate* (New York: The Free Press, 1995).

5. Michael J. Malbin and Thomas L. Gais, *The Day After Reform: Sobering Campaign Finance Lessons from the American States* (Albany, N.Y.: The Rockefeller Institute Press, 1998).

6. Robert K. Goidel, Donald A. Gross, and Todd G. Shields, *Money Matters: Consequences of Campaign Reform in U.S. House Elections* (New York: Rowman & Littlefield, 1999).

7. Clifford W. Brown, Jr., Lynda W. Powell, and Clyde Wilcox, *Serious Money: Fundraising and Contributing in Presidential Nomination Contest* (New York: Cambridge University Press, 1995).

8. David Magleby and Marianne Holt, "The Long Shadow of Soft Money and Issue Advocacy Ads," *Campaigns and Elections* 20, no. 4 (May 1999), 22–27.

9. Anthony Gierzynski, *Legislative Party Campaign Committees in the American States* (Lexington: University Press of Kentucky, 1992); Anthony Gierzynski and David Breaux, "The Financing Role of Parties," in Joel Thompson and Gary Moncrief, editors, *Campaign Finance in State Legislative Elections* (Washington, D.C.: Congressional Quarterly Press, 1998); Paul Herrnson, *Party Campaigning in the 1980s* (Cambridge, Mass.: Harvard University Press, 1988).

10. Darrell M. West and Burdett A. Loomis suggest that this is already happening in key policy debates. See their book *The Sound of Money: How Political Interests Get What They Want* (New York: W. W. Norton, 1999).

11. Trevor Potter, "Issue Advocacy and Express Advocacy," in Anthony Corrado, Thomas E. Mann, Daniel R. Ortiz, Trevor Potter, and Frank J. Sorauf, editors, *Campaign Finance Reform: A Sourcebook* (Washington, D.C.: Brookings Institution Press, 1997).

12. Norman Ornstein, Thomas E. Mann, Paul Taylor, Michael J. Malben, and Anthony Corrado, "Document 9.9," in *Campaign Finance Reform*, 379–384.

13. Ibid., 383.

14. Thomas E. Patterson, *Out of Order* (New York: Alfred A. Knopf, 1993).

Appendix
Detailed Description of Analysis Behind
Figure 4.2

The model included the log of the candidate's and the opponent's spending. A log function was used to model the diminishing marginal returns of campaign spending. Also included were measures for the district's voters' party loyalty (the average vote for the candidate's party), a measure for the perceived competitiveness of the race (the margin of victory in the previous election), an indicator of whether the district elected more than one member of the legislature (that is, whether it was a multimember district or not), and indicator or dummy variables for each of the states. The results for Democratic open-seat candidates was as follows:

Vote percentage = 30.43 + 5.91*(candidate expenditures logged) + 6.06*(opponent expenditures logged) + .34*(average vote in the district) + .07*(previous election margin) – 2.23*(multimember district) + dummy variables for 11 of the 12 states.

The numbers next to each factor indicate how much the vote changes for a unit increase in the factor. So we can use this equation to chart the changes in the vote accompanied by the changes in spending. You can do this by carrying out the calculations in the model. First you plug in the average for all of the other variables and multiply them by their weights. Then you add an amount of candidate spending (logged) and multiply that by the weight for candidate expenditure. Then add them all together to get a vote percentage for that level of spending for the average candidate. Repeat this for different amounts of spending and you have the changes in the vote associated with changes in spending for the average candidate.

Glossary

Bundling: The label given the practice of "bundling" together checks written out to candidates. Individuals or organizations solicit the checks together and present them to the candidate. This way individuals can get around the $1,000 contribution limit, and PACs can circumvent the $5,000 limit since they are not the ones writing the checks—they just collect or bundle them. An example is EMILY'S List, which bundles checks for female candidates.

Challengers: Candidates who run against incumbents.

EMILY's List: An organization that bundles contributions for female candidates. EMILY is an acronym for "early money is like yeast," a phrase that describes the group's purpose of getting seed money to female candidates early in the process to help them raise more money from other sources.

FEC: The Federal Election Commission, charged with overseeing federal elections; established by the 1974 amendments and 1976 amendments to the Federal Election Campaign Act (FECA).

Independent expenditures: Expenditures made in support of opposition of a candidate that are not coordinated with any candidates' campaign. Such expenditures, under *Buckley,* are unlimited.

Issue-advocacy advertisements: Activity by groups or individuals who publicly advocate one side of an issue or set of issues. Issue advertisements are defined by the court as anything that is not "express advocacy" of or opposition to a candidacy.

Open-seat Candidates: Candidates who are running in a race that has no incumbent.

PACs: Political action committees. The term "PAC" or "political action committee" does not appear anywhere in federal law. The FECA, however, encouraged the formation of PACs by allowing for the establishment of multicandidate committees. Such committees must register with the FEC and can contribute up to $5,000 per candidate per election.

Public funding: Government grants to candidates for campaign purposes. Public funding can either be full—if the candidates accept the grants, the grant money is all that they can spend—or partial—candidates can raise money in addition to the public funding grant. Public grants usually specify that the candidates who accept the grants must also abide by spending limits. The federal government has full public funding for presidential general elections and partial funding for the presidential nomination campaign. A number of states have full or partial public funding programs.

Soft money: Campaign money that is not regulated by federal law. Where political parties are concerned, soft money is those funds used by national party committees to pay for the federal portion of state and local party campaign expenses. The money is thus regulated by state laws—which in many states are much more lax than federal law.

References

Abramowitz, Alan I. 1989. "Explaining Senate Election Outcomes," *American Political Science Review* 82: 385–403.

Alexander, Herbert E. 1991. *Reform and Reality: The Financing of State and Local Campaigns* (New York: The Twentieth Century Fund Press).

Alexander, Herbert E. 1992. *Financing Politics: Money, Elections, and Political Reform*, fourth edition (Washington, D.C.: Congressional Quarterly Press).

Biersack, Robert, Paul S. Herrnson, and Clyde Wilcox. 1994. *Risky Business? PAC Decisionmaking in Congressional Elections* (New York: M. E. Sharpe).

Box-Steffensmeier, Janet M., and Jay K. Dow. 1992. "Campaign Contributions in an Unregulated Setting: An Analysis of the 1984 and 1986 California Assembly Elections." *Western Political Quarterly* 45: 609–628.

Breaux, David A., and Anthony Gierzynski. 1991. "'It's Money that Matters': Campaign Expenditures in State Legislative Primaries." *Legislative Studies Quarterly* 16: 429–443.

Brown, Clifford W. Jr., Lynda W. Powell, and Clyde Wilcox. 1995. *Serious Money: Fundraising and Contributing in Presidential Nomination Contest* (New York: Cambridge University Press).

Caldeira, Gregory A., and Samuel C. Patterson. 1982. "Bringing Home the Votes: Electoral Outcomes in State Legislative Races." *Political Behavior* 4: 33–67.

Corrado, Anthony. 1992. *Creative Campaigning: PACs and the Presidential Selection Process* (Boulder, Colo.: Westview Press).

Corrado, Anthony, Thomas E. Mann, Daniel R. Ortiz, Trevor Potter, and Frank J. Sorauf, editors. 1997. *Campaign Finance Reform: A Sourcebook* (Washington, D.C.: Brookings Institution Press).

Dahl, Robert A. 1961. *Who Governs?* (New Haven, Conn.: Yale University Press).

_____. 1989. *Democracy and Its Critics* (New Haven, Conn.: Yale University Press).

Drew, Elizabeth. 1997. *Whatever It Takes: The Real Struggle for Political Power in America* (New York: Viking).

Gais, Thomas. 1998. *Improper Influence: Campaign Finance Law, Political Interest Groups, and the Problem of Equality* (Ann Arbor: University of Michigan Press).

Gierzynski, Anthony. 1992. *Legislative Party Campaign Committees in the American States* (Lexington: University Press of Kentucky).

_____. 1998. "A Framework for the Study of Campaign Finance," in Joel A. Thompson and Gary F. Moncrief, editors, *Campaign Finance in State Legislative Elections* (Washington, D.C.: Congressional Quarterly Press).

Gierzynski, Anthony, and David A. Breaux. 1991. "Money and Votes in State Legislative Elections." *Legislative Studies Quarterly* 16: 203–217.

_____. 1996. "Legislative Elections and the Importance of Money." *Legislative Studies Quarterly* 21: 337–357.

Gierzynski, Anthony, Paul Kleppner, and James Lewis. 1998. "Money or the Machine: Money and Votes in Chicago Aldermanic Elections." *American Politics Quarterly* 26: 160–173.

Giles, Michael W., and Anita Pritchard. 1985. "Campaign Expenditures and Legislative Elections in Florida." *Legislative Studies Quarterly* 10: 71–88.

Goidel, Robert K., Donald A. Gross, and Todd G. Shields. 1999. *Money Matters: Consequences of Campaign Finance Reforms in U.S. House Elections* (New York: Rowman & Littlefied).

Green, Donald Philip, and Jonathan S. Krasno. 1988. "Salvation for the Spendthrift Incumbent: Reestimating the Effects of Campaign Spending in House Elections." *American Journal of Political Science* 32: 884–907.

Grenzke, Janet M. 1989. "PACs and the Congressional Supermarket: the Currency Is Complex." *American Journal of Political Science* 33: 1–24.

Hall, Richard L., and Frank W. Wayman. 1990. "Buying Time: Moneyed Interests and the Mobilization Bias in Congressional Elections." *American Political Science Review* 84: 797–820.

Herrnson, Paul S. 1998. *Congressional Elections: Campaigning at Home and in Washington,* second edition (Washington, D.C.: Congressional Quarterly Press).

Jacobson, Gary C. 1980. *Money in Congressional Elections* (New Haven, Conn.: Yale University Press).

_____. 1990. "The Effects of Campaign Spending in House Elections: New Evidence for Old Arguments." *American Journal of Political Science* 34: 334–362.

Jewell, Malcolm E., and William E. Cassie. 1998. "Can Legislative Campaign Finance Systems Be Reformed?" in Joel A. Thompson and Gary F. Moncrief, editors, *Campaign Finance in State Legislative Elections* (Washington, D.C.: Congressional Quarterly Press).

Jones, Ruth S. 1981. "State Public Campaign Finance: Implications for Partisan Politics." *American Journal of Political Science* 25: 342–361.

Jones, Ruth S., and Thomas J. Borris. 1985. "Strategic Contributing in Legislative Campaigns: The Case of Minnesota." *Legislative Studies Quarterly* 10: 89–105.

Jones, Ruth S., and Anne H. Hopkins. 1985. "State Campaign Fund Raising: Targets and Response." *Journal of Politics* 47: 433–449.

Langbein, Laura I., and Mark A. Lotwis. 1990. "The Political Efficacy of Lobbying and Money: Gun Control in the U.S. House, 1986." *Legislative Studies Quarterly* 15: 413–440,

Malbin, Michael J., and Thomas L. Gais. 1998. *The Day After Reform: Sobering Campaign Finance Lessons from the American States* (Albany, N.Y.: The Rockefeller Institute Press, 1998).

Moorehouse, Sarah M. 1990. "Money Versus Party Effort: Nominating for Governor." *American Journal of Political Science* 34: 706–724.

Patterson, Samuel C. 1982. "Campaign Spending in Contests for Governors." *Western Political Quarterly* 35: 457–477.

Schattschneider, E. E. 1960. *The Semi-Sovereign People: A Realist's View of Democracy in America* (New York: Holt, Rinehart and Winston).

Sorauf, Frank J. 1988. *Money in American Elections* (Glenview, Ill.: Scott, Foresman and Company).

Sorauf, Frank J. 1992. *Inside Campaign Finance: Myths and Realities* (New Haven: Yale University Press).

Squire, Peverill. 1992. "Challenger Profile and Gubernatorial Elections" *Western Political Quarterly* 45: 125–142.

Stewart, Charles III. 1989. "A Sequential Model of U.S. Senate Elections." *Legislative Studies Quarterly* 14: 567–601.

Thomas, Scott J. 1989. "Do Incumbent Expenditures Matter?" *Journal of Politics* 51: 965–976.

Thompson, Joel A., and Gary F. Moncrief, editors. 1998. *Campaign Finance in State Legislative Elections* (Washington, D.C.: Congressional Quarterly Press).

Tucker, Harvey J., and Ronald E. Weber. 1987. "State Legislative Election Outcomes: Contextual Effects and Legislative Performance Effects." *Legislative Studies Quarterly* 12: 537–553.

Verba, Sidney, Kay Lehman Schlozman, and Henry E. Brady. 1995. *Voice and Equality: Civic Volunteerism in American Politics* (Cambridge, Mass.: Harvard University Press, 1995).

Welch, William P. 1976. "The Effectiveness of Expenditures in State Legislative Races." *American Politics Quarterly* 4: 336–356.

West, Darrell M., and Burdett A. Loomis. 1999. *The Sound of Money: How Political Interests Get What They Want* (New York: W. W. Norton & Company).

Wright, John R. 1990. "Contributions, Lobbying, and Committee Voting in the U.S. House of Representatives." *American Political Science Review* 84: 417–438.

Zisk, Betty H. 1987. *Money, Media, and the Grass Roots: State Ballot Issues and the Electoral Process* (Newbury Park, Calif.: Sage Publications).

Index